God's Gift

How to Be a Good Black Woman to a Strong Black Man

By Angela Freeman

God's Gift: How to Be a Good Black Woman to a Strong Black Man

Copyright © 2012-2013 by Angela Freeman

All rights reserved. No part of this book may be reproduced or transmitted in any form or by any means without written permission from the author.

ISBN 978-0-615-76706-2

Dedication

God's Gift is dedicated to Black women in America who have yet to discover the power in their own femininity, and the Black men who remain patiently dedicated.

Table of Contents

Commentary from a Black Man by M. Mwandishi	7
Foreword by Omowale Mayasa	9
Preface	17
Introduction	19
Chapter 1: The Life of a Black Man	21
Chapter 2: Home is His Refuge	29
Chapter 3: Words Have Power	37
Chapter 4: Cooperation	53
Chapter 5: Nourishing Your Man	63
Chapter 6: Sensual Healing	83
Chapter 7: Nurturing His Children	95
Chapter 8: Healing the Family	105
Chapter 9: Divine Beauty	117
Chapter 10: Do Good Men Cheat?	133
Chapter 11: If You Can't Get Along in Peace	139
Chapter 12: Review	149
Chapter 13: Conclusion	153
Special Thanks!	155

Commentary from a Black Man

By Manduzi Mwandishi

Do Not Read This Book... Study It! Have book club meetings. Discuss it with your family and friends. Why do I say this? God's Gift is not your average relationship jargon. It is one of the greatest tools of this generation. The experience shared will provide women of all ages with the knowledge and wisdom to develop and/or maintain the families necessary to rebuild and revitalize the Black Community.

The Akan of West Afrika say, "Only a wise person can solve a difficult problem." The Ancestors have heard our cries. The Torch has been lit and the path has been blazed. God's Gift is that path. The path to peaceful harmonious unions. The path to matrimony.

Foreword

By Omowale Mayasa

According to the Merriam-Webster Dictionary, warfare is defined as:

1. Military operations between enemies: an activity undertaken by a political unit (as a nation) to weaken or destroy another.

2. Struggle between competing entities.

Although this definition rings true, I have a question. Does warfare entail mutual hostility or is it only considered warfare as long as one party attacks?

I'm asking what may appear to be silly questions to get your wheels turning. If you don't think you have an enemy but are being attacked, are you in a war? If you are being attacked and you do not fight back, are you at war? Of course you are in a war!

What these definitions do not tell you is warfare does not have to be mutual or consensual. Warfare is not based on the volleying of barrages, a tennis-like exchange. Warfare is based on the domination or elimination of one group by another through tactical means.

Congratulations! By virtue of purchasing this book you have accepted our enemy's declaration of war, and you have decided to fight back! You either sincerely recognize the need to save your relationship, or keep your thriving Black relationship strong. This is an act of warfare!

We have been fooled into thinking we are each other's enemy. We have become the "Struggle between competing entities". We are not in competition with each other. We have the same enemy! As minor as you think the act of keeping your relationship intact is, remember that an act of warfare is "an activity undertaken by a political unit (as a nation) to weaken or destroy another".

As Black women and men, we are the beginnings of a nation. Nations are a collection of families on a given land with means to feed, clothe, shelter and protect themselves. Keeping our families intact makes it easier to strengthen our areas of weakness.

"If you do not understand white supremacy (racism)-what it is, and how it works- everything else that you understand, will only confuse you"

~ Neely Fuller, Jr. (1971).

Thanks to great Afrikan minds like Dr. Neely Fuller, Jr. and Dr. Frances Cress Welsing, we know for a fact that white people are the global minority and they know it as well.

In order for whites to maintain their genetic survival they came up with a system known as Racism/white-supremacy (I prefer the term "white-domination"). To control the population of the non-white people of the planet, they have devised a diabolical plot to regulate our numbers. This is done by attacking us in overt and covert manners in nine areas of people activity:

1. Economics
2. Education
3. Entertainment
4. Labor
5. Law
6. Politics
7. Religion
8. Sex (Reproduction)
9. War

These nine areas are used to make us ignorant, poor, docile and powerless (and ultimately extinct) by means of trickery and manipulation.

A nation can rise no higher than its women. Although that may seem unfair, it is very critical that you recognize the importance of being the conduit of continued Black existence. It is critical that you recognize the importance of being the first nurse, nurturer and teacher. There is strength in these feminine qualities, and it is how you are divinely made. Truly God's gift.

While you are naturally doing these things, please believe that your good Black man is doing what is divinely mandated of him. We are doing our best under the current circumstances. With your assistance, and our combined efforts we have no choice but to be great (as a nation).

As a real Black man, my only option as a mate is the Black woman, and I have no reservations about that. I know my duties are to provide for and protect my Black family. When my abilities to perform my duties are compromised, I do my best to not put the entire burden on the Black woman. As a Black man I know the Black woman is not my enemy.

Real Black men do not intentionally or indirectly bring harm to the Black woman. A real Black man has long-term plans for his Black family. A real Black man does not waste the Black woman's time selling her dreams. A real Black man can handle constructive criticism (not nagging) from his Black woman. A real Black man does not run at the first sign of trouble. Overall, a real Black man is responsible and accountable. We are often lumped into the category of Black males but aside from looking similar and having the same genitalia, we are two totally different beings!

Thank you Sister for standing up and fighting the good fight and we **WILL** be victorious!!!

Abibifahodie! (Afrikan/Black Liberation)

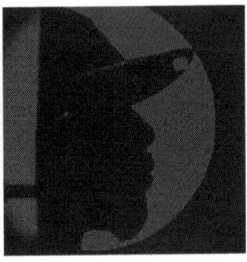

"Complement" Lyrics

By Omowale "Ambassador O" Mayasa of United Front

Spoken Word:
Goddess it's obvious,
This devil got us,
At each other's throats,
Like we don't need each other,
Just to stay afloat.
I took a solemn oath:
I wouldn't abandon you,
Be a man for you,
Stand for you,
Let it bang for you.
Be omnipresent,
Setting the standard,
For our children.
Livin' life in the likeness and image,
Of ourselves.
By us and for us,
In the wilderness and hell of North America.

Verse 1:
Goddess incarnate,
Orisha of my heart,
My reflection,
My lifeline,
My all-spark,
My conscience,
The battery in my back,
The clip to my ratchet,
When I'm on the attack. (Blaaaaat!)
Make a house into a home,
Escape madness in our palace.
The warmth of her embrace,
Focuses my malice.
We know the enemy,
And it's many faces,
And their many motives to try to decimate us.
One is separation,
I don't wanna vision that anxiety.
Literally, for the life of me,
I'd rather die than be,
With tha otha white meat.
Some brothas like to sightsee;
Sayin' they like variety.
Invalid,
But that's a cop out,
And he won't see the light.
Black woman got the most variety,
Cuz there's no phenotype.
That's neither here nor there,
Let me make it clear,
I don't just gotta...
I wanna love you.
Yes, let's take it there.

Chorus:
Brothas seekin' out your Compliments,
You should only look at one continent.
Brotha seekin' out your Compliment?
You should only look at one continent.
Nevermind the geographic location.
When you look at her, God,
You know where she from.
Look at that hair, Sun.
Look at her, damn Sun...
Nahmsayin??

Verse 2:
Don't get it twisted,
I respect yah intellect too,
Nah, Queen this isn't just sexual.
Love and respect is due.
But I'm a man.
When words fail to be adequate,
All I Can Say Is "Damn!!"
In the relationship,
I'll be the anchor,
You the sail.
Only through mis-communication can we fail.
My business is your business.
When I get big headed you let me know I'm trippin' and give
Forgiveness.
I'd be lyin',
If I ain't wanna wring yah neck sometimes.
But in the bigger pic,
I'd be killin' sunshine.
Say It with Me,
Abibifahodie (Afrikan/Black Liberation)!
Aye,

Yes meh lady,
That is the only aim.
As we build,
Being examples for the village,
Keeping the family peace,
And punishing the wicked,
If I come home with blood on my hands,
You already know what it is,
And who it was.
Let's mash!

Chorus:
Brothas seeking out your complements,
You should only look at one continent.
Brotha seeking out your complement?
You should only look at one continent.
Our goals are aligned,
Homes fortified.
Let's hold the line.
Let's hold the line.
I live for you;
You live for me.
Ain't no mystery.
Ain't no mystery.

Spoken Word:
So in a nutshell,
I'm compelled,
To spell it out,
Yell it out,
To the world,
My black woman,
My black pearl,
Many have tried,

But have been denied.
Access to heaven is for heavenly bodies,
And reserved for Gods.
My heart pumps blood,
So love floats in my hemoglobin.
I'd give you my life if you needed it.
I would be your donor.
And this is far from over.

Preface

This book was written out of sheer necessity. Until recently, I was constantly being asked for recommendations for books on improving Black family life. I would respond with an extensive list of generic books that gave useful tips, but lacked vital information because they were not written for a Black audience. After receiving my long, subpar list of self-help books, a friend made the suggestion that I should just write one good book to make it easy. As much as I wanted to protest, I saw her point.

Black women have been under attack more than any other race of women. There is no question, we have been damaged and lured away from our true African character. We need publications that specifically address our unique needs, without the addition of corny gimmicks or unrealistic advice.

I approached writing this book as if I were speaking to a little sister or one of my younger cousins. I included every lesson I wish I would've been told as a child instead of having to learn the hard way. I did not write in a harsh, condescending manner, but I made the language very direct so the points would not be missed.

Often Black women avoid focusing on our own self-improvement by pointing out the flaws of Black men. Although Black men have a massive amount of work to do, that is considered off topic in this book. God's Gift is solely focused on improving the character of Black women. It operates off the assumption that you have wisely chosen a strong man with good character who is committed to you.

It didn't take me a long time to write God's Gift because I already had a good idea of what we (Black women) need to hear. Like many of you, I used to live my life modeling myself after what I was told a Black woman should be. After a while I realized my rendition of a "strong Black woman/Independent woman" was not what kept a family together. In fact, it helped to tear it apart. Acting in that manner did not make me anywhere near as valuable as I assumed. I began to redefine what real strength was and how this different perspective fit into the reality of Black womanhood in America. Once it became clear to me, my happiness and success improved exponentially and I was able to build a happy home.

Due to the many days and nights I spent desperately pondering this subject during my younger years, the words flowed easily from my heart to these pages as soon as I started to write. After you read this book, reread it. Let the various points marinate in your mind. Much of it may be completely opposite of what you have tried before. This means that you will get much different results! I pray this information is of benefit to you and your family.

"The Liberation Struggle can no longer afford the luxury of failed relationships. Sincere, committed parties must figure out how to best work with one another, 'cause there's plenty of work for everybody."

~ Heru Ptah MeriTef

Introduction

"Where are all the good Black men at?" Everywhere! I know very few women who have never encountered a good man. We get good men, and then we lose them. The question is why? Why do men spend a lifetime with certain women, but can't stand to be around others longer than a few months? Where do we go wrong?

Many times it doesn't matter how much money the woman makes. Often, facial features and body dimensions aren't the main factors. What matters most to mature, family-oriented Black men is who will give them peace! Men want tranquil women they don't have to fight with constantly. Women who respect men. Women with charisma and character. Women who would never ask, "Where are all the good Black men at?"

Many single women would love to pacify themselves, believing there is no particular recipe for relating to all men. They will quickly (and incorrectly) state, "All men are different." This takes the burden of blame and responsibility off of them. I'll let you in on a little secret; most men are not as different as you may think. They all have an innate need to be admired, desired and respected. Decent Black men want to protect and provide for women who need them in their lives. Men need to be needed.

The independent facade of the majority of Black women, coupled with extremely confrontational attitudes has sentenced us to a life filled with temporary relationships. We pretend we don't need our men while we wear the bitter scars of loneliness. It's time to mature and change our attitudes. Is "doing bad all by yourself" really working for you?

God's Gift is a manual on loving strong Black men. The philosophy of this book will not work on underdeveloped men. Assuming you have made a good choice in a mate, following the very basic steps provided in God's Gift will create a positive change in your relationship from day one. This book will not only help you to be a better wife and mother, it will help you grow as a person. It will make you happier, healthier and more confident. Femininity will radiate from you. You will have that "special something" that makes men stay for a lifetime. After all, you are God's gift!

Chapter One: The Life of a Black Man

Imagine waking up bright and early, ready to go to work to earn a living for your family. You shower and put on a crisp suit and tie. As you rush to leave and open the door, you suddenly hear the jingle of the beads in your baby girl's hair. You see her running towards you at about one hundred miles per hour. She crashes into you, then puts her hands around your legs and reminds you not to leave without saying goodbye. You pick her up and kiss her sweet little cocoa brown face and tell her to be good in school.

It's a beautiful autumn day. The sky is blue and leaves are beginning to change colors. There is a cool breeze in the air. This is a welcome change from the 100 degree weather you endured all summer. You hop in the new car you were recently able to purchase after working overtime for several months. Your job is cool. At least it pays the bills. You are proud to be able to take care of your family. Too bad your father isn't alive to see you. You begin to drive and make sure to be careful about stopping at all the stop signs. The cops in your neighborhood have been harassing people left and right lately. As you roll down the street, you suddenly see red and blue lights flashing. Here we go again!

As you pull over, you call your wife to let her know what's happening. You consider keeping her on the line as a witness in case anything goes wrong, but she says she has to get the children off to school. A sloppy, fat, white police officer waddles to the side of the car and asks you to roll down your window. The smell of sweaty wet dog fills the air. After asking if there is a problem, you comply and give him your license and registration. He doesn't bother to answer your question, but you already know the routine. He asks if you have any warrants. You say no, but of course he doesn't believe you. He goes to run your license while you wait. You really hope this doesn't make you late for work.... again. Suddenly you notice two more cars pull up. What is going on? The other cops get out of their car and ask you to step out of the vehicle. You ask what the problem is. One of them tells you to shut up and demands to search your car. You know that you shouldn't give him permission, but since you have to get to work you don't protest. They make you sit on the dirty curb while they go through every inch of your car. They seem to be upset that they can't find anything illegal. You feel like a chump as everyone drives by staring and pointing, assuming you are some lowlife criminal. The cops take their time and make you wait another 20 minutes while they talk and keep searching places they have already searched. You figure that you might as well go ahead and call in late to work. Finally they let you go, telling you to be more careful next time.

You rush into work and clock in hoping you haven't missed much. This will probably be another ten hour day. At lunch time, you go to grab some fast food. Your doctor says you need to stop eating out so much because you are on the verge of having Diabetes and your blood pressure is high too. What choice do you have though? You don't know how to cook and your wife isn't going to pack you a lunch. Fast food is convenient. You look pretty healthy, so the doctor is probably just overreacting. As you get on the elevator to exit the building you shake your head at the white woman next to you holding onto her purse for dear life. It's like she doesn't realize that you both work at the same place, making the same money. She doesn't have anything you want. It's amazing how afraid white women act, until they want sex, then all that trepidation magically disappears. You just shake your head as you get off of the elevator.

On your way to the restaurant you see a few nice looking sisters. Since your mother raised you to be a gentleman you say, "Hi sisters, how you doing today?" They just roll their eyes and keep walking. A brother can't get any love today! You walk in the restaurant and there is Chun Li pretending she doesn't speak English. She has no problem counting cash though. Profiting off of Black people is a language she understands very well. You order your regular, General Tso chicken with noodles, two egg rolls and a Mountain Dew. You grab your food and rush back to work. The day is halfway over. Good!

When you get to your desk you see a note from your supervisor asking you to come to his office. You hurry up and eat since your break is almost over, then walk over to his office to see what's up. You knock on the door and he tells you to come in. You sit down wondering what this is about. He states you've been late quite a bit lately. You explain that this is only the third time in four months. The other two were because of car trouble, but you have a new car now. The tardiness today was out of your control. He says "Regardless, we have to maintain strict standards or everyone will start coming in as they please. We're going to have to let you go. You can go on and get your things from your desk."

You stare at him for a moment to be sure that you heard him right. You have been working here for three years. The last few months you have voluntarily worked 60 hours a week to help with the extra workload. You were up for a promotion in a few months. Are they really worried about a few late days? They should be glad you came in at all! As the news sinks in, you leave to retrieve your things from your desk. You see a security guard standing outside of the office. Are they serious? The guard escorts you to get your things, watching you as if you are going to steal something or go on a shooting spree. He walks you all the way to the sidewalk outside, where he remembers to take your badge. As you walk to your shiny new car you wonder how in the world you are going to tell your wife you lost your job. She's going to be beyond angry. You stop at the store and buy her some flowers. Maybe that will soften the blow.

You come home at the normal time. You see your wife starting to "cook dinner" which basically means making instant mashed potatoes and heating up a few cans of vegetables to go along with the pre-cooked rotisserie chicken she bought from the grocery store's deli. You hand her the flowers as you kiss her softly on the cheek. She gives you a half smile, sets the flowers on the counter and continues "cooking". You ignore her ungratefulness because you know what you are about to tell her. You look away and say, "Baby you wouldn't believe what happened after that cop pulled me over this morning!" She puts a hand on her hip and stares at you. You calmly explain everything that happened ending with you losing your job. You hope she sees that your manhood has obviously been bruised and that she'll have sympathy for you. Instead she says, "Well I don't know what you want me to do. I'm not in the business of supporting no lazy Negros." You remind her that the two of you have a little money saved up so you should be fine while you look for another job. She says, "You ain't spending up all of MY money! You got one month to find a job or you can go stay with your momma. I can do bad all by myself!"

You look at her amazed. Is this the same woman you helped to put through college? Is this the same woman you supported while she stayed home with the children until they were school aged? Does she remember that you've spent the last decade raising a child that isn't even yours right along with your own biological children? Has she lost her natural Black mind? Obviously! She sets the table, minus one place. She looks at you coldly and reminds you, "If you don't work, you don't eat." You knew she wouldn't take it well, but she is being ridiculous.... and saying all this in front of your children. As you look at your family, all the children are sitting sadly with their heads hanging down. You decide to leave before you do something you'll regret. She is really pushing you tonight. You open the door, and like clockwork, you hear the sound of little beads jingling as you are almost tackled from behind. "Don't go daddy, you can have my food if you want", your little angel said with tears rolling down her cheeks. You pick up your baby girl, wipe her tears and kiss her face. Seeing her crying makes you so angry, you feel like choking your wife. Instead you hug your daughter tight and tell her to go eat. You put her down gently and lock the door. KFC is sure to be packed this time of day, maybe you should get pizza?

God's Gift

This story isn't a far stretch from what many good Black men endure regularly. Not only do they deal with racism outside the home, they find no empathy inside the home. We all say that we want a good, strong Black man; but we don't know how to act when we get one. We don't take care of him properly. We rarely speak a good word to our spouse to encourage him to keep pressing on. In fact, we are often on the attack. Many of us think we are God's gift while we treat our men like we are God's curse.

Are Black men perfect? Not even close! That doesn't really matter though because this book isn't about them. It's about us. Wise people understand that the only person one can change is one's self. With that in mind, this book will attempt to answer questions that Black women should be asking ourselves daily like: What can we do to improve the condition of the Black family? What did our grandmothers know and understand that we don't? How did everything go so wrong? These and many other questions will be examined in the pages to come.

Feminism

One thing we must understand as Black women is that the feminist movement really hurt the stability of Black families. Until then, Black women were standing side by side with our men fighting white supremacy. At some point, we let our historic enemies fool us into thinking that our war was with our men, not our former enslavers. They even gave us incentives like welfare to convince us to get rid of our men. Many of us left the real struggle behind and became divided against our partners. A house divided cannot stand.

White females have the right to be feminists. History proves how terribly they have been treated by their males. Rape, beating, murder and neglect have always been commonplace for them. In contrast, until very recently, Black men always showed great respect for their women. It wasn't until the crack epidemic (planned by the government) and hip hop music (controlled by Zionists) that we really lost this basic respect on a massive scale. We never had any reason to be feminists or to turn against our men. The males responsible for making our lives Hell were white.

There is nothing feminine about feminism. Feminism is just a destructive way of competing with men instead of truly valuing the female principle by cooperating. Our unique nature is powerful and no less important than the masculine principle. Our lives become much more balanced when we are in tune with our nature instead of challenging our complements (Black men) for their position. When we return to being the goddesses we were born to be, our communities will improve overnight. We need the creativity, nurturing and feminine strength that can only come from Black women.

The majority of today's women are repulsed by the concept of femininity because of how it is portrayed in misogynistic European culture. The oppression of women has always been integral to white civilization. Since integration we have been groomed to believe that being feminine means pretending to be weak, dumbing ourselves down and being taken advantage of (the typical characteristics of white females). This is the exact opposite of African culture. From our vantage point, exuding femininity has nothing to do with weakness. African women are strong, brilliant and resourceful. A centered Black woman is not afraid to take care of her family with a virtuous, loving spirit. To a healthy Black mind, femininity signifies grace, wisdom and dignity. Do not lower yourself by following European standards of womanhood. However, remain humble about your God-given strengths and talents.

Self-Refinement

It seems like we've just about hit rock bottom as a community. There is nowhere to go but up. Yet, we aren't able to move up until we get a few things straight within ourselves. Once we become the kind of women we should be, we will be well within our rights to hold Black men to higher standards. However, as long as we are in the mud with them, we have little right to point the finger.

You will not find any male-bashing in this book. The focus of this book is strictly you and I, Black women. I purposely wrote this to be as one-sided as possible. Also, you won't necessarily learn how to get a man in this book- that's easy. We've all been successful getting a man at some point. I want to help you keep your strong man once you find him. That's the hard part because it requires dedication and consistency.

"God's Gift" is about becoming the total package. It shows you how to be indispensable and irreplaceable. There are no crazy gimmicks such as thinking like a man while trying to carry yourself as a woman. I won't ask you to mail me any tithes to make your wish come true. I won't try to give you "game". We've been playing around too long. My only goal is to teach you a few life skills that will not only impress your man, but will elevate your entire family. We must return to our natural selves.

Some of the topics we will explore include:

- How to be a competent homemaker
- How to communicate effectively
- How to be cooperative
- What to feed our families

- How to wholesomely improve our sex lives
- Tips for child rearing, natural health, beauty, tact & attitude
- When to let go

The solutions to our problems are holistic. The philosophy of this book is easy to apply if you honestly love and respect the man you've chosen to be with. These are things our mothers should have taught us a long time ago. It's never too late to learn.

Let us begin.

Chapter Two: Home is His Refuge

Black men must have a haven to get away from the racist, hostile society we live in. He needs to be able to come home, relax, eat a good meal, play with his children and enjoy his wife's affection. This refuge allows him to recuperate mentally, spiritually and physically. His home should be tranquil and relatively quiet. It should be clean and smell good. Everything should be organized and have a place. There should not be anyone living there who constantly nit-picks and argues with him. This ruins his oasis.

Many women run their man away because they refuse to let him enjoy peace at home. We have been groomed to believe that domestic chores should be split 50/50, especially if we work outside of the home. While this would be nice, it's not always realistic. Men come home with the desire to rest, kick up their feet and recover for the next day. If he is a wise man, he will help out a little with chores and children. However, I wouldn't count on it. Black women (who have not been ruined by feminism) have a never-ending desire to nest. We are always cleaning, beautifying, teaching and creating a heaven. This is the Black woman's nature - not the Black man's.

Often these differences can make our men appear selfish and trifling. The truth is that the male and female natures just haven't caught up with modern life. Historically, Black women weren't gone 40+ hours a week. When we were, we had extended family to help us. The nuclear family structure makes things much more difficult. Have you ever watched a documentary on traditional African life? Did you notice the men relaxing by the tree drinking palm wine after completing the day's work, while the women are working hard to make dinner? Now picture your man with his beverage watching the game with his friends while you make dinner. Same concept. It may be annoying, but try not to break the peace. Black men are decent, kind people. I'm sure he doesn't want to see you stressed out. Try having a loving heart-to-heart conversation if you become too overwhelmed. This doesn't mean you should start endless complaining for the heck of it, or because you are lazy. Try improving how you manage your time. Become more organized. Care of the home is primarily your job, even if he does help out.

Homemaking skills are an asset! These skills have become rare; therefore it sets you apart from the crowd to know how to manage a household. Never let anyone make you feel that knowing how to cook, clean or sew is a bad thing. Just consider it another addition to your life's resume. The people who laugh at these skills are usually ignorant, miserable or both.

It is vital to keep your home clean to promote good health and peace of mind. A dirty house says a lot about who you are. It is hard to function in a clutter-filled environment. Not only is it mentally disturbing, but it is easy to misplace or trip over things, not to mention being prone to accumulate more germs. Many people look polished on the outside, but are completely unbalanced on the inside. As a result, their internal mess and dissatisfaction spill over into the home, putting it on display for everyone to see.

Homemaking is not just about cleaning, though keeping things tidy is important. It is also about atmosphere. Your home should feel like home. I used to have two friends. They both had really nice, clean homes. One loved homemaking and decor. Her home felt warm and welcoming when you came in. This positive energy made you want to relax and stay awhile. The other friend did not enjoy homemaking. I think she probably resented it. Her home always felt slightly cold and tense, no matter how beautiful the architecture was. I never wanted to stay too long.

The friend with the warm home chose to be very happy in life. She had a positive attitude which expressed itself in the home environment and everything she did. The other friend was not genuinely happy. Sometimes she seemed downright bitter, angry and unkind. This also could be observed in her home and everything she touched. It doesn't matter if you live in a castle or a hut, your attitude, the vibe of your relationship, the love or lack thereof all help to create your home's atmosphere.

Taking care of home also means catering to your man whenever possible. This is not old fashioned or degrading. Men don't necessarily like being "mothered" but they do enjoy being pampered. There is a difference. Making him feel special strokes his ego and makes him desire you even more. Most things that we consider "spoiling" don't take much time. Foot rubs, breakfast in bed, running bath water, buying a thoughtful gift or initiating a spontaneous rendezvous can take less than 30 minutes. Filling a tub with water, for instance, takes about 5 minutes. Don't believe the hype, real women love to "spoil" their man.

Helpful Hint: *In healthy relationships men and women gladly serve each other. Women serve men by providing comfort in various ways. Men serve women through protection, security and sustenance, among other things. Both roles are intertwined and equally necessary. Never be ashamed to be in service to your man. Devotion is a beautiful virtue.*

You should take pride in serving your entire family. What better way is there to show your love then by presenting them with a hot plate of home cooked food? Try to eat at the dining room table if at all possible. Go the extra mile and make it pretty; presentation is important. Buy colorful placemats and matching dishes. Candles and fresh flowers look great as table décor. This doesn't take much time or money, yet it creates ambiance. Be creative. Always serve the king of the castle first, then your children, then yourself. This is a symbol of selflessness and love. Keep dinnertime conversation non-stressful. Take this opportunity to learn about each other's day and what is going on in each other's lives. Connect with each other. Never argue while eating a meal.

To keep the peace, you may have to use what I call "righteous deception" at times. Righteous deception is not the same as lying. I am not an advocate of lying because it ruins trust. In order for a relationship to last, you must have absolute confidence in the other person. You never know when there could be a life and death situation. You better be able to trust your spouse and vice versa! Never mislead him about anything important.

Righteous deception is a concept that requires cleverness, wittiness, and omission. This is true feminine "girl power". It means you may look like you're paying attention when you're not. You may appear intrigued when you are bored. You might say "yes dear" to pacify him until you have time to strategize something better. You might wear a revealing outfit to distract him from something. You might make him an extra good dinner to butter him up. Most often, you will make him think your idea was his. These things are necessary sometimes to keep a joyful spirit in the home. Besides that, it's fun! Righteous deception is always done out of love, not treachery. We will discuss this further in later chapters.

Keeping house might seem monotonous, but you should approach it gratefully and graciously. Remember, some people are sleeping outside tonight. They wish they had a roof over their head. Take joy in creating beauty and peace in your space.

Helpful Hint: Most men are happy as long as they have a clean home, peace and quiet, tasty food and physical satisfaction. They have very simple desires, unlike us. You don't have to jump through hoops to keep your man happy. Just be sure those basics are covered.

Housekeeping Tips:

- Your house should always be no more than 5-15 minutes away from being spotless. If someone were to call you with some sort of crisis and needed to come over unexpectedly, it should take no more than 15 minutes to put things away, vacuum, dust, etc. to have your home ready to receive guests. If it takes you longer than that, your home is out of order.
- Himalayan Salt Lamps purify the air naturally and help with dust accumulation. They also provide a very pretty glow in a room.
- Keeping a home clean is not as hard as it seems if you follow common sense rules. If you take something, put it back in its place. Make the bed as soon as you get up. Clean out the tub as soon as you finish. Wash the dishes (or load the dishwasher) as soon as you are finished eating. Respect your clothes and put them away. Don't procrastinate if you see something that needs to be done.
- Aromatherapy is a great way to create different moods in the home. You can use citrus for energy, lavender for relaxation, etc. Always use 100% pure essential oils, not cheap perfume oils.
- Start teaching children to clean as soon as they can walk, and don't present it as a chore, make it a fun activity. Start by showing them how to put their toys away.

- Try using baking soda and essential oils instead of commercial carpet fresheners to freshen the carpet.
- Change your attitude about housework. If you (and the children) do a little every day, then you rarely have to do a lot. This soon becomes a habit. Before long, dirt and clutter will begin to annoy you. You will clean automatically.
- Greet your man at the door with a smile and a hug whenever possible. Allow the children to greet their father, but be sure he has time to relax before you all start burdening him with issues and problems.
- Preparing an aromatherapy bath as soon as he gets home allows him to relax and transition from work to home. This puts his mind at ease and enables him to be more patient and pleasant with you and the children.
- Take off your shoes when you enter you home. There is no telling what you may have stepped in outside, but the one thing that is guaranteed is that you picked up a lot of nasty germs. It makes no sense to drag those germs into a clean home. Have a cozy nook for people to take off their shoes, along with a rack or neat space to leave them. Try not to just throw them in a huge shoe pile. Respect the material possessions you've been blessed with. It would be very convenient to have a pretty basket on display with booties or socks available for people who may not be wearing socks. This is not expensive. You can buy surgical style booties to fit over the shoes of any workers who may not be able to take off their shoes while working in the home. Everyone else should take them off upon entering- NO EXCEPTIONS.
- Always have a snack available for surprise guests. This could be pie, a tray with fruit, cheese and crackers, or cookie dough kept in the freezer just in case. Always be prepared to be a good hostess.
- Do not keep your toothbrush in the bathroom. Everyone should keep their toothbrush in their bedroom. Stores have plenty of styles of decorative toothbrush holders now. You can get one that will match your bedroom. There are nasty germs floating around your bathroom, no matter how often you clean it. That room is no place for your toothbrush to be stored.

- Try to keep your toilet lid closed, especially when flushing. When you flush, waste particles go airborne and get on everything, towels, walls, and your toothbrush- if you didn't use my last tip. The proper procedure is to close the lid, flush; open the lid to make sure you didn't leave any surprises, and then close the lid again. Guests usually won't do this, but if your family makes this a habit it will significantly decrease the amount of miscellaneous crud in your bathroom area.
- Try wiping out the fridge every week before you go grocery shopping. This prevents dirt buildup and allows you to see what you need to buy and what should be thrown out.
- The tub should be wiped out after every use. You can't get clean in a dirty tub.
- Everyone should use new towels and washcloths every day (or every bath if you bathe more than once daily). It is unhygienic to try to clean your body with a dirty rag. It is also not the best idea to put a dirty towel on a freshly cleaned body. This creates a lot of laundry, but that is fine because you should be washing towels as their own load anyway. It is not good to wash towels with the clothes you've been wearing outside around countless germs and infections.
- Speaking of laundry, you should also have a separate load for dish towels. You would not want to dry off a plate with a pair of boxer briefs, so you should not be washing your towels with underwear or outerwear. All those germs, discharges, and random nastiness will go right to the towels you use on your dishes. Yes, I know that's a nasty thought. Change these towels daily as well. I once knew a woman who used laundry detergent to wash dishes. I asked why she did that, because it seemed odd to me. She said it kept the rag from smelling sour. (Insert shocked face here) You should NOT be using dish rags long enough for them to become smelly and mildewed.
- Beds should be made as soon as you get up. Not only does it make bedrooms look clean instantly, it also makes you less likely to lie back down. Sheets should be changed at least once a week. This may be more in warm weather if you sweat. They should be changed any and every time there is sexual activity. They should be changed as much as possible during colds or illness.

- Wipe off the stove when you are finished cooking. Don't let dirt accumulate.
- Trash cans should ideally be wiped down every time you take the trash out. For me this is every night. I can't stand trash sitting in my home. This keeps the home fresh and prevents nasty buildup in the trash cans.
- Disinfect all doorknobs once a week, after having guests, or whenever there is illness in the home. We often forget about doorknobs, but they are a haven for germs.
- Eliminate clutter by giving things away, throwing things away, and having adequate storage. Storage should be attractive and add to the decor of the house. It should never be a bunch of Rubbermaid bins visibly stacked in the corner. Find a nice way to hide them. I do a spring cleaning and an autumn cleaning. This way I am constantly analyzing what I do and don't need. You'd be surprised what we hold on to. Let it go!
- This would be a good time to discuss live plants. Not only do they make your house look much better and add life, but they actually clean and oxygenate your home. This is great for overall health, allergies and respiratory issues. Live plants can be a mental pick-me-up similar to having a pet, but with none of the germs. You can start as small as an herb garden, a miniature lemon tree, a cactus, etc. Ivy grows well in low light. Just experiment and see what fits your personality. Plants need to be nurtured though, so be attentive.
- If you really hate cleaning, play some music. It makes the process less painful and it helps the time go by faster.
- Be cautious who you allow in your home. Allowing a free flow of people can bring in roaches, bed bugs and other uninvited guests.
- Don't look sloppy at home. If you wear jogging suits make sure they fit, they match, they don't have holes, and they flatter your body. Also, keep your hair done and always look pretty.
- To get rid of ants, sprinkle cinnamon essential oil in a line near your doorways. They hate the smell and will turn away.
- If you have an issue with bugs even when your home is clean (from neighbors, etc.) sprinkle Borax laundry detergent on your floors. This will kill waterbugs, roaches, etc.

A good way to make your home his refuge is to be very generous about giving your man private time. There are times when a man likes to be alone with his thoughts. Sometimes he may need to relax by pursuing a hobby (martial arts, video games, reading, etc.). Although he should not neglect the family's needs, avoid crowding his space. Instead of resenting his desire for solitude, try looking for the bright side of the situation. For instance, you could let the children take a nap and do something that you enjoy while he is away.

<u>Helpful Hint</u>: Many times we get into a relationship and stop pursuing our own interests and hobbies. This can make you quite dissatisfied with your life, as well as cause you to be a bore. Continue to pursue your interests, study and make time for yourself. You can't bring joy to your family if you are not fulfilled and happy within.

Don't think of housekeeping as "slaving away." Think of it as beautifying your home and increasing your family's quality of life. The art of homemaking is something you never stop learning. There is always a new idea or new product that you may benefit from. Browse through magazines and online articles for decor ideas and helpful tips. The most important thing is the respect and love between family members, especially you and your spouse.

<u>Helpful Hint</u>: Let everyone who enters your home feel the genuine love and contentment. Many times they might not have any of their own, so to be able to share yours is a blessing.

Chapter Three: Words Have Power

The most powerful forces in modern Black relationships are the words that come out of the mouths of Black women. This alone can make or break a union. More often than not, our words are aggressive, negative and disrespectful. This misbehavior has become almost automatic, meaning that usually we are not even aware of how destructive our speech is to our men and children.

Changing your thinking is the first step towards improving the way you choose to communicate. America's media influence has been destructively ingrained in our subconscious mind. The Zionist controlled hip hop industry has skillfully trained Black men to disrespect and violate us. Meanwhile, the Zionist controlled movie industry has trained us to fight against our men whenever possible. Because we live in a severely dysfunctional society, many of us never had the opportunity to see loving Black relationships. There were no other examples besides what was featured on the television. We began to assume that the idea of a functional Black relationship was just a fairy tale, or that on rare occasions when we did find love it would end tragically. In most movies and television series geared towards Black women, we were shown that Black men were a burden and were not worth our time. Loving Black men always led to pain, betrayal and misery. We fell for the propaganda.

Had our parents and grandparents done their jobs more effectively, we would have been taught about the upstanding Black men who fought for us and loved us dearly. We would have grown to admire Nat Turner instead of Lil' Wayne, Henry Highland Garnet instead of Tyler Perry, Elijah Muhammad instead of Steve Harvey and Robert F. Williams instead of Snoop Dogg. This would have given us a much healthier mindset, making it easy to respect Black men. This knowledge would have also given us a higher degree of Black pride and racial loyalty. Because we lacked examples of strong Black men, we were forced to look up to extremely unqualified specimens. The concept of true Black manhood became a mystery to us.

Be this as it may, we are adults now. Black women must grow into maturity and develop the ability to critique ourselves and claim responsibility for our role in the destruction of the Black family. We must begin to think positively about the people who look like us. Black women must go out of our own way to start being respectful and caring towards our men. Either we are in this together, or we aren't. If you feel we aren't, then you might as well stop reading now. However, if we are in this together then let's look at how we should speak to our men.

Silence & Indirectness

This may be a hard pill to swallow, but the most effective way to start changing the spirit in which you communicate is to spend more time being quiet. In general, women speak way too much. Even I am guilty of this at times. Because many of us have never grown up with non-effeminized male figures, we aren't aware of the differences in male and female personalities. We treat our spouses the same way we treat our female friends. We expect long frivolous conversation and gossip. That's not what real men do - at least not with women.

Black men love peace and quiet at home. If your man isn't in the mood to talk, allow him to enjoy silence. Don't keep bothering him by asking what he's thinking. If he wants you to know he will tell you. Everyone has a right to their own private thoughts. Try to avoid asking what he's feeling. Men hate that. As a matter of fact, try not to ask too many questions in general. Most men dislike being questioned. We may be asking questions out of pure curiosity but they may feel like it's an interrogation. It's better to let him come to you to say what's on his mind. Let him know that you're there for him by saying, "It seems like you have something on your mind. I'm here if you want to talk about it." Those words let him know you care without prying or pushing.

If he does confide in you, ask probing questions (this is different than prying) to keep him talking. This works because it strokes his ego. He will believe that you are really into the conversation because of how fascinating he is. Say things like "then what happened?", "so what did you do then?", "why did they do that?" or "so what did you say then?" These phrases should be said with extreme interest, excitement or amazement in your voice. A bored, monotone voice doesn't work.

By closing our mouths we are able to listen carefully to our spouse. We learn his likes and dislikes. We discover his motivations, strengths and weaknesses. By closing our mouths we can begin to see what he needs and how we can best serve him. You help a man grow to his full potential by understanding his vision in comparison to his reality. You can never do this based on wild assumptions made without listening to him directly. You must know where he wants to go, how he intends to go there, what he has to help him get there, what obstacles might make it more difficult for him to get there, and what he needs from you to get there.

Silence also gives us time to really think about what we want to say and if it's even worth saying. You should always think before you speak. Let your words play out in your mind. Are you saying something important? How is your spirit? How is your tone? Is there a better way to word it? Consider all these things before opening your mouth. It may seem like a lot to do every time you want to say something. Good! That means you'll probably talk much less as I previously suggested (smile).

<u>Helpful Hint:</u> Words have power, but so does silence. Everything doesn't require a response. You don't always have to have the last word. Sometimes silence speaks much louder than words.

When you do talk to him about serious matters, pick a good time. Common sense says you will get bad results if you try to hash things out during the Superbowl or while he's trying to get the top score on a video game. Unfortunately, many women are rude enough to try to interrupt men when their attention is obviously elsewhere. The funny thing is that we get mad when the man tells us to get out of the way or ignores us completely. Please remember that men prioritize things differently than we do. That means the game might be more important to him than discussing him leaving the toilet seat up again. It also means that he may forget things that you say, because he didn't place the same level of importance on it that you did. Always pick a good, quiet time to discuss things. Dinnertime would be much better, assuming you don't sit in front of the television during mealtimes.

When we do talk to our men, we should do so with a gentle, loving spirit. Do not come at your man as an opponent- at least not if you want to keep him. Your man is not your child so don't speak to him like a mother. He will not react well to being spoken to "man-to-man" either. Always allow him to stay on his throne while you stay on your pedestal. Never discuss issues when you are too angry to do so calmly and rationally. These methods are all counterproductive. Being overly direct and aggressive is never a good approach in a relationship. As a woman, your power is in your femininity and the appearance of submission. If you don't use this power, your home life will never be as good as it could be.

For example, very often men will veto a woman's direct advice almost automatically because he feels that he is well able to make decisions on his own. Determining solutions is a part of his job as the leader of the home. It is against his nature to submit to a female, although men may make an exception if the woman is an elder. That's just an aspect of the male character that we must maneuver around. Watch a wise woman in action. She will subtly spoil her man all day long, smile at him, compliment his masculinity, present him with a meal, and then gently imply an idea or desire through "pillow talk" that night. Remember, it is important to be subtle! You don't want him to realize he's being buttered up or kindly conned. If you treat him well on a daily basis he shouldn't even be able to notice the difference. Under these conditions he is far more likely to say yes or at least bounce your idea around in his mind. Frequently, his ego will then convince him that your idea was something he thought up on his own. This is the ultimate win because he will have no reason to rebel against his own idea. That is the genius of femininity. Checkmate!

Controlling Anger

So what do you do to release your anger when you feel he is acting stubborn, ignorant, belligerent, etc.? I'll tell you what not to do! Never make the mistake of disclosing too much to your friends and family. You should both be able to expect some level of privacy. Find trusted elders with a proven track record, if you must seek counsel. This is a degenerate society so transparency is not always the best option. Secondly, it is your job to keep the image of your man pristine. The world is against Black men. He is constantly stereotyped and presented negatively. Don't join that club, it is treasonous. Other people do not forgive and forget as quickly as you do. When you move on, your associates will still look at your man harshly. Thirdly, this too shall pass! We as women will always find something to complain about. Nine times out of ten it will be over with and soon forgotten.

But there are several things that you can do to feel better. Keep a journal to write in. Write down every nasty thing you want to say. Write down every time he gets on your nerves. Take no prisoners. Expose all his trifling madness. Put it away for a few days then come back and re-read it. Was the situation really that bad? Hopefully it wasn't. I would recommend that you keep this journal locked up or just shred the pages once you've moved on. Most of the angry words you wrote, you probably didn't even mean. You wouldn't want him to find it and have his feelings hurt or ego bruised. That is why writing is a much better option than speaking out of anger. You can get rid of written words. Spoken words last forever.

Exercise is also a great option to relieve anger. Go for a walk, run on a treadmill or better yet, assault a punching bag for a while. This is very positive because it keeps you in shape and quiets your spirit. It also wears you out enough to take away some of your energy to argue. If you still want to quarrel, then as a last resort, go to a shooting range if that's your thing. Just make sure that you are out of ammo before you come home! Just a joke, but seriously, do whatever you need to do to keep your peace of mind intact.

If punching bags and shooting ranges aren't your thing, learn to bake fresh bread. I know you are probably thinking I have lost my mind after reading this suggestion, but stay with me. You have to really beat and kneed bread to get it to come out right. When you are angry you have lots of strength to work the dough well. Let all of your anger and aggression go into preparing those loaves of bread. It will be some of the best bread you've ever tasted. After a while your man will begin to put two and two together and figure out that if you are making bread, he did something wrong. You won't even have to say it. He will be well aware of it and either stay out of your way, apologize or come to a satisfactory solution.

Likewise, cleaning the house thoroughly takes a lot of energy and will wear you out if you do it correctly. All of the reaching, scrubbing, wiping, folding, etc. could actually be classified as exercise. You can even use a soothing aromatherapy grade essential oil (lemon, lavender, mint, geranium, tangerine) to help elevate your mood as well as to deodorize and disinfect. A clean home always makes you feel better.

Sometimes it may be better to write a letter stating your feelings. He can't argue and fuss with a letter. Be sure the letter doesn't seem angry or disrespectful, just state your position, any hurt feelings and what you think an adequate solution is. Include any details that you feel are important. Calmly ask him to read it at his convenience, hand it to him and walk away. Let him read it when he's ready. He may not open up a dialogue about it, but rest assured that you were heard.

Generally the woman sets the tone of the home. If you are radiant and deal with your family intelligently, you elevate the spirit of your home. If you are angry and abusive, your household will be Hell. You can't control your man's behavior but you can control how you react to it. Never stoop to his level when he is being unreasonable. If he's taking out his frustration on you try reacting with tenderness instead of returning hostility. He may be dealing with things that you don't know about. It takes time and patience to stop taking his words, emotional distance and attitudes personally. However, understanding makes all the difference when trying to maintain a peaceful, loving environment. He'll come around soon enough, and when he does he will respect you even more for your maturity.

Don't Belittle

Today's Black woman seems to belittle her man without even realizing it. Again, I think it goes back to media influence which was our main example of how to relate to our men. Both our tone of voice and wording often suggests irritation, tension or outright belligerence. We tend to not talk to men as though they are our respected and beloved partners. We are far more likely to speak to them as adolescents, punks, losers and second class citizens. Many times the most racist of white males can't compete with Black women for malicious disrespect of Black men. That is sad.

Examples of disrespectful things some of us say:
- Shut up!
- I don't care....
- Whatever!
- I'm the one paying the bills anyway....

- You better call Tyrone....
- Don't tell me what to do
- I don't need you!
- Who the F@#$ are you?
- I can do bad by myself...
- Sleep on the couch!
- You ain't my daddy!
- You ain't about nuthin' noway!
- F@#k you!
- ... wit' yo' broke @$$
- Leave me alone!
- Do it yourself.
- You better go to KFC if you're hungry. I ain't cooking.
- N-word, please!
- I don't have to listen to you
- You ain't ballin'
- You can't even hit it right....

I think we've all heard most of these expressions at some point in time. Black men disrespect us just as viciously. It has become a never-ending cycle. This is the unfortunate state of Black America today. It must change. Regardless, don't verbally castrate your man. It is counter-productive and only keeps the cycle going.

> **Helpful Hint:** *Due to our history in this country, Black men crave respect more than any other group of people. Always show the utmost respect in conversations. Always acknowledge that whatever he is saying is relevant and important.*

You don't always have to agree with your man, but you should always maintain a level of decency and respect during debates. Only children and people who think on the level of children maintain no control over their emotions. There is a way to disagree amicably. And don't be silly enough to believe that disagreements must always be settled. There may be things he promotes that you will never believe in. Yet, if you are wise you will discover how to pick your battles wisely and when to concede on those things that don't really matter. Just because you allow him the last word on an issue, doesn't mean you change your mind. It simply means you choose peace.

If you do lose control and say something inappropriate, apologize immediately. Even if he also said something foul, be the bigger person. You can say something such as, "I was wrong to speak to you that way. I shouldn't have said (fill in the blank) and it won't happen again". This is short and sweet and only admits wrongdoing for your disrespect, not for your views. This gives you back your dignity while honoring your spouse. If an argument goes too far and you don't feel the need to apologize for your words, at least express regret that it went to that level. If your man apologizes to you, be sure to accept the apology graciously. It takes humility to apologize, so try not to make it more difficult than it already is. Remember, a healthy relationship takes forgiveness, understanding and support.

Helpful Hint: *Never be afraid to admit you are wrong. Acknowledging wrong doesn't show weakness, it shows maturity and makes a man feel respected.*

Here are some phrases to pacify your man during those times when you don't want to actually say, "I apologize":
- I will definitely give your thoughts the consideration they deserve (they may not deserve consideration so this is a good "righteously deceptive" thing to say).
- I didn't realize you felt that way....
- I'm sorry you feel that way (make sure there is no sarcasm in your voice).
- Thank you for telling me. I didn't realize that.......
- I will do better next time....
- I respect your decision (you can respect it even if you disagree)
- I will be sure not to do that again
- I take responsibility for that.....
- I love you (this is a good diversion if you can slip it in without him noticing your intent)
- You smell good tonight. What cologne are you wearing? (This is also a diversion, but with a slight innuendo in case "I love you" doesn't work. Always be strategic and have a "plan b")

Don't make sarcastic or sly remarks when trying to quell an argument. It will only make things worse by making you appear insincere and making him angrier. Losing control in an argument does not make you look cute. Depending on how severely out of order you become, you may even look like a complete savage or a psycho. Yelling, cussing and physical altercations are not signs of an upright woman.

<u>Helpful Hint:</u> Never argue in public! I repeat, never argue in public or in front of guests. We all make mistakes but do not allow yourself to be knocked off your pedestal. Use creativity instead of aggression. He will love you for it.

One last suggestion is to start keeping your opinions to yourself. You don't have to tell him everything that comes to mind. You don't like his tie? Be glad you don't have to wear it. If he likes it, you should love it. Was he overly aggressive with someone? Be glad it wasn't you behaving in that manner. Is he driving a little too fast? Tighten up your seat belt. If he asks for your opinion, don't hesitate to express it (tactfully). If he doesn't ask, that means he doesn't need it. He probably has an opinion about many of the things that you do. You probably don't want to hear his assessments any more than he wants to hear yours.

Men Don't Submit to Women

Many times men have to hear things from other men. Rarely will they listen to women. This is one of the more perturbing aspects of the male personality. This is also why it's a complete waste of time to try to change a man. Don't waste your breath.

For example, I encouraged my husband to be vegetarian for almost a year. I showed him articles, documentaries, medical studies and delicious meatless recipes that I could make. He made it clear he was not giving up fish. I said fine, and continued making him baked salmon, salmon croquettes, fried tilapia or glazed orange roughy fish two to three days per week, and meatless meals the rest of the time. Then one day we went to a meeting during a religious holiday where we met a distinguished elder. As we ate dinner, the elder disclosed that he was a vegetarian and it was an extremely healthy lifestyle. As we drove home, my husband had the nerve to look at me and say, "You know what? I think that maybe we should be vegetarian. Don't buy any more fish." I didn't know whether to laugh or look out of the window and roll my eyes (out of his sight, of course). So I was able to get my wish, but not because of anything I said or did. He remained a hardcore vegetarian for years until the elder passed away. Now he will eat fish a few times a year. Dear sisters... that is how the mind of a man works. We don't like it, but we must understand it.

The desire and determination to lead is innate in Black men. Unfortunately, it can be damaged by this racist society, including the condescending attitudes of his mother or wife. But this desire, whether active or dormant, is why men rebel so adamantly against submitting to taking advice from or listening to women. As annoying as it is, this slight chauvinism is important to his spirit. Therefore, it is up to us to find a way to work around it while leaving his manhood intact. Otherwise we weaken our men, and ultimately our defense, because their role is the protector. This is just one of those things you have to deal with.

Speaking Nicely

It may be a challenge, but we have to start using our words to uplift our men. They can accomplish anything if they know we love them and believe in them. This must be consistently expressed in words and actions. When you speak to your man your tone should be very soft and gentle. You should have a unique inflection in your voice that you use only when you speak to him. You should call him by his name, or by a pet name (baby, sweetie, love, king, sugar, sexual chocolate, Mandingo warrior-god, etc. ... take your pick). To most men, there is no sound sweeter than hearing you say his name (affectionately, not when you are hollering!).

When conversing in private try to sit close to him, look in his eyes admiringly; touch him from time to time. Act absolutely intrigued even if he is boring you to tears. Feel free to stop paying attention to him and go over your grocery list, work on your budget, or plan your to-do list in your mind. Just be sure that you maintain eye contact and nod convincingly every now and then. Throwing in an occasional "yeah" or "I know that's right" doesn't hurt either. He'll never know the difference.

Remember basic etiquette like, "please", "thank you" and "I apologize". If you mess up, there is nothing wrong with telling him, "I'll do better next time". That may be enough to squash a problem before it blows up into an argument. Always be humble, even if he isn't.

Compliment his masculine qualities on a regular basis. It doesn't matter if it's in reference to his physique, his accomplishments, his chivalry, his dreams, his libido or his toughness. Any time that you observe manliness, make it a point to compliment him. This boosts his confidence and satisfies his desire for admiration. Don't worry about him becoming too cocky. Black men should have healthy egos. It helps counter the never ending negativity they have to endure. As long as he doesn't get so arrogant that he starts to degrade you, let his ego grow.

Offer words of encouragement! Never forget that the whole world is telling him what he is incapable of. Become that angelic voice telling him that the sky is the limit. Be positive! Let him know that you have faith in his abilities and that you will be there through thick and thin. Be sincere. Men need to hear these things.

You should also be sympathetic when necessary. A friend of mine told me recently that some women will sit with their spouse watching a movie about a man who is struggling. She may cry for that character and cheer him on throughout the movie. However her spouse may have gone through even more, and still be going through it, but he will get no sympathy from that woman. This scenario is ridiculous. A woman should be a support system for her man. He should get more empathy and concern than anyone else in your life. We have to do better.

Try not to tell him things like "There's nothing to worry about" or "there's nothing to fear". These phrases make it seem like you are more courageous than him; therefore, you might have more manhood than he does. This can appear to be demeaning and unattractive. The best choice of words simply assures him that bright, sunny days are coming soon and he is capable of weathering this storm.

<u>Helpful Hint:</u> Avoid using emasculating words like "little" when referring to him, his ideas or his accomplishments. Little is not a very manly word and tends to minimize him and his accomplishments. It sounds insulting. Instead use

words like "big" or "great". It makes a difference.

When you must let him know that he needs to improve in an area, say it nicely and don't accuse. Try phrases like: "It would help me so much if you could please (insert activity here)" or "I need you to (insert activity here). Thank you love, I really appreciate it" or "Thank you so much for (insert activity here), but is it possible for you to (insert activity here) next time?" Any of those phrases sound better than saying, "Would you get up off your lazy butt and take out the garbage?!? This house smells worse than yo' momma's!" See the difference? I'm just saying.

If you are not sure about what pleasant, loving, ego-stroking conversation sounds like, buy an Anita Baker cd. If your man is 25 or younger you can probably recite a whole verse word for word and get away with it. Her lyrics are beautiful and full of good material that you can use.

Nice Wording includes:
- Honey, could you please (fill in the blank)
- Thank you baby.
- I really appreciate that.
- Do you need anything?
- Can I get you anything?
- What can I do for you?
- I apologize. I was wrong.
- I'm with you.
- I need you.
- Things would be so much harder without you.
- You are so good to me.
- I appreciate you so much.
- Thanks for your help.
- I really admire how hard you work.
- You are a great father.
- Thanks for helping me with that. You are so strong!

When you don't make it a priority to speak nicely and honor your man, you leave your relationship very vulnerable. Most "home wrecking women" do not win over a man by sex alone. Most of them know how to be very feminine and submissive. They make the man feel wanted and needed. While their wives are cussing them out on the phone for forgetting to pick up his socks again, the wise mistress is straddled on top of him in new lingerie, massaging his back and whispering to him how big his muscles are. As your husband, he definitely has a duty to live up to whatever standards of faithfulness you have agreed upon. As his wife, you certainly have a duty to fulfill his needs and not push him into degeneracy, irresponsibility and dishonesty.

Gratitude

I often sit quietly and observe people, especially how they interact in their relationships. It helps me to learn lessons to improve my marriage. Elders are few and far between nowadays, so keep your eyes open to see living examples of what works and what doesn't. Don't repeat other people's mistakes. Let me share a true story with you.

One day I was visiting at one of my associate's homes. We were discussing what we wanted to do in the future as far as home improvements. I've been rehabbing my home for quite a while now, so I love getting new ideas from people. My associate's home wasn't very organized or "homey" but it was decent. They owned nice things but these things weren't stored well. Everything was in piles on the floor or on top of furniture. While my associate was telling me about all the things that needed to be done to make her home "livable" (it was already livable), her man overheard our conversation. He looked at her with an attitude and snapped, "With what money?" She responded by stating that the house must be updated because everything was old.

What's wrong with this? First, her man is the main bread-winner for the family. He even stepped up to take care of children who are not his biologically. Therefore, she should always praise what he has been able to provide for their family. There is always room for improvement. In fact, constant betterment of the home environment is part of the woman's role. However, you must let him know that what he has provided is sufficient and satisfactory to you as-is. He looked around considering her complaints along with her lack of homemaking and thought about all the money he had already spent, which seemingly amounted to nothing. No one wants to provide for an ungrateful person. This will give even really good men an instant attitude, rightfully so.

You cannot expect someone to want to give you more when you aren't taking care of the many things you already have! Your possessions should be kept clean and organized. Taking care of your things shows that you value them (and the effort it took to acquire them). It is a slap in the face for a man who supports you to come home and see things that he worked to provide not properly put away. Even if you are the one who buys most of your things with your own money, clutter makes the home uncomfortable for the family.

Nobody is perfect and it is easy to be indifferent or ungrateful for our blessings. Someone always has more than us. There is always something new coming out. People judge us based on what we do or don't have. Regardless, we must make a conscious effort to count our blessings daily and show gratitude by telling him how much we appreciate what he does. I will repeat again- men thrive on admiration.

If you consistently show your man appreciation and admiration for the hard work he does (even white collar work can be stressful for a strong-minded Black man), then (and only then) should you be tactfully and femininely asking for extras. You should ask nicely. Never make demands. Again, you may want to softly make your desires known while "basking in the afterglow of love". Generally, when he feels appreciated and sees you valuing the possessions you already have, he will be more inclined to happily give you what you want. Black men want to please a good woman. If yours doesn't, you either made a bad choice in mate selection or (more likely) you need to adjust your attitude. Keep working on it.

Joking Around

Joking is a good way to have fun with your partner. As a matter of fact my husband and I often say things jokingly to each other. We both have thick skin, a very good sense of humor and an extreme level of comfort with one another. Sometimes people are surprised when they see us interact. We laugh a lot. Often we get on the other's nerves so much that even our annoyance becomes a joke. Neither of us has much "act right" so we don't take ourselves too seriously.

However, not everyone is like that. In fact, most are not. You have to know your partner and his limits. Sometimes, too much joking is not good at all. What you intend to be a joke may be highly offensive to a sensitive, serious or uptight spouse. Try not to joke about anything regarding their masculine characteristics. Again, you want to protect their ego. Family jokes or yo' momma jokes may be a touchy subject as well. As always, think before you speak. How would you like it if it was said to you? Are you ready to apologize if he takes it the wrong way? Is it worth the possible drama? Only you can answer those questions.

Chapter Four: Cooperation

    Any strong relationship is built on unity. If you are not working together for the common good of your union, it is doomed to fail. A family is a little kingdom you build from the ground up. Every kingdom has a leader- the king. In a family the leader is the man. We waste time arguing this point. Crazed feminists have made many people question the obvious. I'm going to tell you again, in a healthy, functional family the leader is the man.

    Black women are very strong. We have withstood trauma and difficulty that would've broken any other race of women. We have been raped, beaten, separated from our families, forced to see our loved ones lynched and our men be destroyed. We've been forced to neglect our own babies while we nursed the babies of the demons who tormented us. We cooked for them, cleaned for them and were forced to have babies who were fathered and abandoned by them. It is no wonder we no longer want to submit to authority. It reminds us too much of what we've been striving to overcome.

    We must remember that we have never been under the rule of Black men since we've been on these shores. The white race has been the architect of our pain and misery. Black men are not our enemy or oppressor. They have suffered through the same things we have. They may have failed us in many ways, but we have also failed them. In their confused state, Black men have done many things to hurt us. Make no mistake; all of this was scripted by white people. The Black man does not deserve all of our anger and wrath, especially not our husbands. We need to heal our wounds together.

The modern Black woman often works in direct opposition to Black men and Black manhood. We have been granted privileges in this society that our men will never have. It would be great if we used these advantages to help uplift our men, but usually we use these benefits to keep him down. We are given jobs more easily. We are treated with more respect. We are not as likely to be lynched by the police. The laws are tilted in our favor in terms of custody, child support and many other domestic issues. This has taught us that the white male "has our back" against our natural life partners and logical allies, Black men.

Working Against the Black Family

We must become wiser in the way that we deal with our men. That is the basis of this book. We need to learn to get along, keep the peace and shield each other from the dangers of this society.

For instance, some women will start a petty argument with their man. Then, if their man won't back down and submit to her will, the foolish woman may call the police and make up a story about feeling threatened or being in danger. A few minutes later, the bloodthirsty police officers will arrive with their guns drawn and ready to shoot. One wrong move and the brother is dead, over nothing. Even if he cooperates willingly, it is not unheard of for a cop to make up an excuse to lynch a Black man. This entire scenario could have been avoided if the woman was mature enough to relate to her man wisely and humble herself. I'm not saying that we should never call the police. If you are in real danger of rape, assault or murder by all means call! However, don't risk his life over silly disagreements and nonsense. Any time the police are on the scene, the Black man's life is in danger. Playing these games is pure evil and should never be tolerated.

Another silly thing about some Black women is that we will work against our own interests in order to uphold white supremacy and Black destruction. Black women realize that finding a Black man is made more difficult because of the vicious trend of homosexuality. The ironic thing is that these same women have gay male friends. Most Black women openly support this deathstyle, which is an institution that will someday ensure that our daughters will never have a decent selection of good Black men to choose from. We also tend to blame "straight" men for bringing AIDS into the community. We refuse to face the reality that if a man willingly has sexual contact with another man, he is homosexual. Undercover gay males are the main group of males infecting our community, not straight men. Why should decent Black men take the blame? This does not let sexually irresponsible heterosexuals off the hook, but let's be realistic. Worse yet, we allow these damaged men to have access to our sons, increasing the chances that our sons will be molested and "turned out". Seriously Black woman, we must do better!

Sometimes when a relationship comes to an end, the mother does her best to create as much turmoil as possible. It doesn't matter how much it hurts the children, as long as it also hurts the man. Black women have been known to intentionally keep children away from their father. Many times she'll speak negatively about the father or outright lie on him trying to cause the children to resent him. Every now and then she may even make up false abuse or molestation charges against the man. She does her best to keep them estranged if this will hurt him. Meanwhile, she will tell everyone she knows what a deadbeat he is. To the world, the brother is a no good bum who doesn't love his children. She will fight in court for an inordinate amount of child support in order to financially break him. Once she is awarded some ridiculous payment, she will often spend it on herself while neglecting her children's needs. Once she spends all of the "child support" she will go to the father and tell him the children need new shoes or clothes. If he refuses to give her even more money she will tell their children, "Your daddy doesn't care if you need new shoes and clothes." She makes sure the man knows he has no say in how the child is raised. Sometimes, after all of this, the man finds out that the children are not even his. But remember, he is the bad parent.

These are just a few examples of things that many Black women do which are completely counterproductive to the future of the Black family. We can never get ahead if we don't work together. We each have responsibilities and roles to fulfill. Pointing the finger at each other is useless.

Let Him Lead

So how do we begin to better relate to our men? This is a highly unpopular topic amongst Black women, but number one on the list is you must submit to your man's authority. In order for any unit to achieve success, there must always be order and rank. If he is the president, you are the vice president. If he is the captain, you are the lieutenant. Just because he may have a slightly higher rank doesn't mean you aren't still very important and necessary. Even your children have rank (civilians/private soldiers). Everyone in the family has a job and is worthy of respect and consideration. That being said, he does outrank you in terms of control. He is the family's leader.

> *<u>Helpful Hints:</u> Men and women are 100% equal in terms of their value and rights. However, rights are different than authority. You are not equal in terms of authority. Your input is valued, but his decision is final.*

Submission simply means following the instructions and requests of your man. If he says a room is messy and needs attention, clean it. If he asks you to handle some business, do it. If he says your dress is too short, change clothes. It's pretty cut and dry. It won't kill you to follow instruction. Most of us follow orders every day on our job without question. Submission only becomes a problem when our Black man needs us to do something. Keep in mind that I'm not telling you to submit to just any Black man. No ma'am, certainly not. I am telling you to submit to a serious Black man who has proved his commitment to you by **marrying you**. When you make the decision to marry a man he should have qualities such as honesty, responsibility and a noble character which makes him fit to lead a household. **I do not believe a so-called "boyfriend" has earned any right to your submission and dedication. If he wants the best of you, let him prove himself worthy by marrying you.**

The Black husband is the natural protector of the family and home. A man cannot protect what he doesn't control. I know of a man who advised all women who were under his authority to be home before dark. Many of the ladies felt this was unreasonable and very outdated. They became less diligent as time went on, and started coming home later and later when they could get away with it. One day, one of the young ladies was on her way home at dusk. She decided she wanted some candy. She saw that nightfall was very close, but didn't think a short detour would hurt. The sister ended up being brutally raped on the way home. To add insult to injury, the thug took her precious candy before leaving her. It was only then that she realized the wisdom of the admonishment she was given. Crime had been on the rise, especially at night. The request to be home early was not chauvinistic; it was for her own good. From that moment on, she followed orders. It's tragic that it took such a horrible incident for her to listen.

A defiant woman puts her man in danger. There was a family who lived beside a very uncouth man. He often started problems, especially with the wife. The husband told his wife that whenever the man said anything to her, she should just go in the house. One day the man began speaking very disrespectfully to the woman. Instead of leaving she argued with him and they began cussing each other out. Finally she decided to go inside. When her husband came home she told him that the man cussed her out, conveniently leaving out the rest of the story. This put the husband in the position of having to defend her honor. He went over to talk to the man, but instead the man started swinging. They fought for a while and somehow the husband ended up losing three fingers in the brawl. This could have been avoided if his silly wife had just obeyed her husband.

Expressing Your Views and Getting Your Way

<u>Helpful Hint:</u> There are ways to express your views and get your way at home. In most circumstances, direct confrontation and rebellion are not productive!

Skillful ladies rely on feminine charm, righteous deception (including pillow talk) and patience to get results instead of aggressive tactics. There is a saying that "the man is the head, but the woman is the neck that turns the head any way she wants". There is nothing demeaning about using guile to get your way. We must learn how to be real women in order to peacefully coexist.

In any successful relationship there are rules that must be followed. Household rules are based on religious or philosophical beliefs, societal norms and the needs of the family. Rules are necessary to establish order. Every house has its own way of doing things. Everyone who enters your home should be bound by your house rules. If the children see you following the rules and the instructions of the father, they are far more likely to do the same. They will be disciplined and give you fewer problems. If they see you being disrespectful, corrupt and rebellious they will follow your lead. You and the father will both lose respect in their eyes. That means threatening; "I'm going to tell your dad when he gets home" will not carry much weight. Once that happens, the family is in trouble. Set a good example.

The members of your family should be working towards a common goal. If everyone wants to do their own thing and go in different directions, the family won't get anywhere. Success requires everyone's cooperation. Cooperation demands that everyone must work together in harmony and support each other. One person's strengths cover another person's weakness. Everyone's talents are utilized. Everyone contributes and moves as a unit. The leader must keep everyone in the family on track.

Being a submissive woman means following instructions humbly and happily. If you have an attitude or complaint every time you are asked to do something, you are not submissive. If you get offended every time he asks for a glass of water, you are not submissive. If you get around to doing things when you want to do them instead of when he needs them done, you are not submissive. If you are in constant disagreement, you are not submissive. We all disagree from time to time. The fact remains that you cannot constantly be at odds with each other and still be successful. Love can only flourish where there is agreement and harmony. Let's not kid ourselves. We must improve our attitudes.

This subject may be difficult to accept, but, you will see as time goes on that things run much smoother when there is order. Your family will be much happier. There can be no peace in the midst of chaos. As you get out of your man's way, you will begin to see your man in a beautiful new light. Besides, men will only take so much. Once they wake up and realize they don't have to tolerate our bad behavior we will have no choice but to improve. No other race of women has so much of an issue allowing their men to be men. Our hesitation to do so is very disrespectful. It is helping to keep us an underclass.

Unintentional Sabotage

What if your man has been irresponsible in the past? How can you just trust in him again without hesitation? Should you submit to a man who makes bad decisions? At first glance, this seems like a difficult position to be in. But realistically, I doubt that your judgment is bad enough to choose an incapable man as a life partner. Maybe the real problem is your perception.

The power of suggestion is a dynamic thing. Advertisers use it frequently to control our subconscious desires to make us want to buy their products. The media uses innuendo to control the way the masses think and act. We can use suggestion in a positive or negative way. A suggestion can be as simple as a look of disgust, a leading question or body posture. You may or may not be aware when you send out these messages, but if you doubt that your man is a capable leader, your suggestions will definitely be harmful.

Women tend to be very arrogant when it comes to forgetting our own mistakes. In our mind, we always do things the best way. When men make a mistake it sticks out in our minds, because we have conveniently forgotten the last 999 mistakes we've made. Over time this allows us to develop a very negative image of our man. It feels as if they can't do anything right! We forget that mistakes are mere learning opportunities. Some of us lose so much faith in our man that we prefer to do everything ourselves. Then we are angry when we become overwhelmed and stressed out. Always keep in mind that there is more than one way to do things.

Once we form a disrespectful, unjust image of his so-called incompetence in our minds, we start to project it onto him. This can be very detrimental. Men tend to form a large portion of their self-image through their mate's opinions of them. We know our man better than anyone, so how we see him holds a lot of weight. If you show your partner that you think he's irresponsible, he probably will be. If you say he never helps around the house, he won't. If you accuse him of cheating when he's not, one day he might. They call this a "self-fulfilling prophecy" and it happens all the time. This projection of doubt is more powerful than you realize. This is why a man will often struggle with failure the entire time he's with one woman, but as soon he gets with a new woman he excels. You are very influential.

Focus on your man's talents and positive attributes. Say uplifting things about your man! Expect wonderful things from him. The more you focus on the things he does well, the less crucial his flaws become in your eyes. Instead of focusing on his lack of "romance", focus on how well he treats you daily. Instead of focusing on his tardiness, focus on how hard he works to provide for the family. There is always a better way to look at things. Your reality can change based on your perception.

Most times Black women need to mind our own business. If he has a task or chore to do, let him do it! Stop hanging around waiting for him to mess up. Don't sneak around making sure that he did what he was supposed to do. He is a grown man. If something doesn't get done, he will have to deal with the consequences. Not trusting him to fulfill his responsibilities is very emasculating. Some males never grow up because from the start, their mothers are always going behind them fixing things for them. When their mother gets tired of them, they find another woman willing to "take care of him". Males will become men when we expect and allow them to be. Running behind them gives them an excuse to be negligent. If you have a responsible man, checking up on him is just getting in his way. We need to step back, put ourselves in "time out" and let our men show us what they can do.

Once we decide to let go of the control, we have to be fair enough to allow him to make mistakes. As he becomes accustomed to living in his proper role, there has to be a learning curve. He is no more perfect than we are. When we force ourselves to see our men as capable human beings who are going to make errors at times, we give them the space needed to excel. The only people who never make mistakes are the ones who aren't doing anything. Sometimes it makes all the difference in the world for a man to know that his woman believes in him. That positivity can make him go out and move mountains to make a better life for his family. The Black man's potential is infinite if it is nurtured by his woman.

The Black woman in America usually operates out of fear. We have seen and experienced some of the most horrific things imaginable which have led many of us to have phobias that make us unreasonable at times. It is our fears, especially fear of abandonment, loneliness, failure, poverty and embarrassment that create the negative attitudes which spill over into our relationships. The irony is that often it is these fearful attitudes that attract these hardships into our lives. Whatever energy you send out into the universe comes back exponentially. In order to be cooperative you must work on having a more positive attitude. Be grateful for your many blessings. Live in the moment instead of worrying about the future all the time. You must know that no matter what happens in your life, you will endure.

Once you stop being so critical of your man, start asking his opinion about things. Trust him enough to allow him to solve some of your problems for you. Strive to become interdependent with him, not independent from him. No man wants to hear you whine about your problems for hours. He wants to find a viable solution. Helping you overcome various issues makes him feel needed and manly. It may also give you simplified solutions that you would've never thought of. Have faith in your man's wisdom. He just might surprise you.

You and Him Against the World

You should always have your husband's back in the public. Do not openly side with other people against him. Do not speak negatively about him to others. Demand that people respect him. Don't let other people, including family and friends, go too far with jokes and comments about him. Don't hesitate to firmly defend him, even against his own family. If you are a unit, you must work together to keep each other's respect and dignity intact. Do not willingly allow anyone to violate his image or tarnish his reputation. This brings both of you honor in the eyes of others.

Regardless to whom or what, you are a team.

Chapter Five: Nourishing Your Man

Most Black women are so busy competing with men for the right to be known as "independent" that they never stop to think about the powerful role they are abandoning. Being a homemaker (whether you have outside employment or not) literally gives you the power of life and death. This is not mindless feminist rambling, its reality. Most Black men who don't die from violence, are dying from preventable lifestyle related diseases such as heart attack, stroke, diabetes and cancer. All of these diseases are preventable. That's where you come in.

Sister, you are the nurse, doctor, dietician, chef and herbalist of your home. Your job description includes nurturing and nourishing. It is up to you to study and make sure your family is given the best in terms of food and medicine. Actually, food and medicine are interchangeable words because food is your medicine when you begin living right. We must begin taking this responsibility seriously. We can heal a nation, or we can continue killing our nation through neglect.

It is tragic that so few Black women know how to cook. Sometimes our mothers weren't there to teach us. Sometimes our mothers felt that school was more important than learning domestic skills. Sometimes we thought we were too good to "slave in the kitchen". The biggest believers in male superiority are women. That is why we don't want to be "stuck" engaging in anything related to the female role. We don't want to cook, clean, take care of a husband or a child. Anything (masculine) a man can do, we think we can do better. We feel that anything feminine is demeaning and unimportant. Being a mother and a real wife (one who does her duty) doesn't seem appealing to the majority of us.

The rejection of feminine expression is appalling. Women and men complement each other. Black women contribute grace, intuition, morality, pleasure, peace and creativity. Life is very bland without a woman's touch. Homemaking is not a sign of laziness or a lack of drive. It is an art form. It is a science. It is a way to express yourself and ensure the psychological, spiritual and physical wellbeing of your family - especially when living in a degenerate, racist and chaotic country like America. There are few ways to express your love to your family better than creating a delicious homemade meal for them.

To my independent sisters, you cannot say you are independent if you don't have basic survival skills. Does it really matter how big your house is if you can barely make a grilled cheese sandwich on your shiny new stainless steel stove? What would happen to you if all the restaurants closed? True independence should at least include learning to how cook, clean and sew for yourself.

Why would you want to be independent anyway? The true goal for anyone reading this book is interdependence. That means that you have a decent partner who you cooperate with to raise a stable family and ensure a prosperous future for your descendants. If you are truly independent, you don't need a man and are prepared to live alone indefinitely. Sounds like a miserable life to me.

The Causes of Illness

Why are Black people so sick? It doesn't seem to matter what our age group, socio-economic status, gender or any other demographic classification is. We are in bad shape as a so-called race!

Part of this is due to the inordinate amount of fast food, processed food and junk food we consume. A generation ago, Black women were the best cooks in America. We knew how to season food to taste better than anything you could get at a restaurant. As bad as the "soul food" diet was, it did contain a lot of fresh herbs and vegetables. Back in the day, some of us even had gardens to grow our own produce. We had not become hooked on the convenience of microwaves yet, because we knew microwaved food tasted horrible. We were also smart enough to be concerned about the health effects of "nuking" our food. Getting a "happy meal" was a real treat because it happened so rarely. Most times, if you wanted a hamburger, your mother pulled ground beef out of the refrigerator. You weren't going to get a toy to go along with your soggy "Wonderbread" burger. But even without the toy, life was good.

If you fast forward to today it is the complete opposite. Processed foods laced with MSG, High Fructose Corn Syrup (HFCS) and artificial flavorings have allowed us to forget how to use healing herbs to flavor our food. The most some of us know how to do is sprinkle on some "Lawry's" which is a terrible choice. We use microwaves daily. Some of us would burn the house down trying to heat up food in an oven. Our home life is last on the priority list, so not only do we live off "happy meals" and "value meals", we can't even fry chicken. We think a dead white male named Colonel Sanders can fry chicken better than we (Black women) can. BLASPHEMY!

Our poor children have it the worst and there's nothing they can do about it. A typical day might go something like this:

Breakfast: Sugary chemical filled cereal with milk containing growth hormones and other chemicals that cause them to be "hyperactive".

School Lunch: Low quality cheese pizza with a side of canned vegetables, tater tots or some other nutrition-less, unappetizing food that doesn't compliment pizza at all. Don't forget the tooth decaying, high fructose corn syrup filled soda pop or chocolate milk.

Snack: Flaming hot chips? Cookies? Candy bar?

Dinner: Fast food chicken-like nuggets with fake honey, french fries, and another soda. Oh yeah, and if they are lucky, a dessert from the dollar menu.

Is it any wonder they are suffering from type 2 diabetes, obesity, asthma, so-called hyperactivity, etc.? Whose fault is this, mothers? Who are we going to try to blame? We need to point at ourselves. We should know better and do better.

So once you decide to take control of your family's diet, then what? You have to make a long term commitment to health. This is a never-ending process. There is always something else to learn. Our foods are so overly processed and packed with chemicals and toxins that you can rest assured your diet will never be pristine. However, you can make it as good as possible by making most of your food from scratch.

What is a Whole Food Plant-Based Diet?

It is what is advocated in this book. This is a transitional diet that lessens the meat and processed foods you consume, which helps detoxify your body. It requires you to cook your food! This way of eating is the epitome of moderation, and is easy to stick to. The way most of us currently eat forces us to ingest an enormous amount of chemical additives, pesticides, refined white foods (sugar, rice, flour), low fiber foods, high calorie foods and nutrient-poor foods. This creates a host of problems.

First on the list is constipation. The body is made to eliminate toxic substances quickly and regularly. When we are constipated all of those poisons back up and eventually enter the bloodstream (autointoxication). From there your body tries it's hardest to get rid of these substances through other channels such as the skin (acne), the nose (snot), the mouth (phlegm), etc. Constipation is often the cause of bad body odor and bad breath. This toxic buildup is the root of many major illnesses. How do you know if you are constipated? You should have a bowel movement for every meal you consume. If you eat twice a day you should have two bowel movements daily. If you eat four times a day you should have four bowel movements daily. If your body is not eliminating on this level, you have issues to address. Chapter 8 gives ideas on how to treat this; however, you must begin with diet.

Another issue is mucous build up. The body produces mucous naturally for use as a lubricant (among other things). That is normal. However, certain foods cause the body to produce unnatural, thick mucus. This toxic mucous goes hand in hand with inflammation and inflammatory disease such as arthritis, sinusitis, colitis, asthma, dermatitis, IBS, Parkinson's, lupus, hepatitis, diverticulitis, and the list goes on. Any disorder ending with -itis suggests inflammation and noxious mucous. The main dietary culprits in mucous formation are sugar, meat and dairy products. These types of foods need to be kept at a reasonable (minimal) level. I am not telling you your man must be vegan. I am telling you to use good judgment when selecting food. These foods should be gradually decreased to reduce stress on the body. Don't try giving everything up at once. You may consult chapter 8 for a recipe for "spicy lemonade" which helps to cleanse accumulated mucous when taken daily or used for fasting.

Pay close attention to your man, but be very incognito. Don't appear to be some overbearing weirdo. You should know approximately how often he uses the bathroom, how long it takes, how frequently he coughs, if it's a dry or wet cough, how he smells, etc. You have to know these things in order to know when something is wrong. I usually know when my husband is getting sick before he feels any discomfort. Then I can jump into action and fix it before the illness takes hold. These things make you invaluable and give you goddess status in his eyes. Men hate to be sick (and are big babies when they are sick)! Save yourself the headache with knowledge and prevention.

The best way to start feeding your family this way is by adding non-processed whole foods to your meals. Most whole foods don't come in packaging (fruits, veggies, bulk grains). Realistically, there will be times when you will eat processed food. If you aren't sure what foods are best to eat, read the label. If there is anything listed that you can't pronounce, don't eat it until you research and find out exactly what it is. You have to be proactive. The best foods have only a few simple ingredients, all of which you should be familiar with (flour, water, butter, etc.). Allow good foods to replace the junk.

For example:

Breakfast: *Instead of feeding your children sugary cereal, make them Apple Spice Oatmeal and Banana Pancakes (recipes found later in this chapter) with a side of sliced fruit and a glass of lemonade sweetened with honey.*

Lunch: *Make a nice romaine salad to go along with their sandwich. While you are at it, swap the white bread for whole wheat bread. Pack 100% fruit juice or water instead of soda.*

Snack: *Banana chips or organic (oven baked) potato chips seasoned with sea salt make far better snacks than Dorito's or Flaming Hot Cheetos.*

Dinner: *Add lots of veggie side dishes to round out the meal. Whole wheat cheddar biscuits would be nice as well. For dessert make a fruit and (organic) yogurt parfait with granola or a fruit smoothie.*

Doesn't this sound far better than the child's menu we discussed earlier? This healthier menu will allow a child to excel in school, have lots of energy to play and to be healthy. The same concept works for your man as well. The beauty of eating this way is that healthy whole foods are much lower in calories, fat and added sugar than processed food. This allows you to eat much more, so you are not hungry. These foods are packed with water, fiber and nutrients. This is not a fad diet; it is a lifestyle change that is not just sustainable, but actually enjoyable. The main thing is getting back in the kitchen.

What are considered whole foods? Fresh fruit and vegetables, minimally processed grains and beans are all examples. Even things like cage free organic eggs, organic dairy, organic meat and small wild caught fish can have a place (in moderation). Do not eat pork (sausage, hot dogs, pepperoni, bacon, pork rinds, etc.) or scavengers (shrimp, lobsters, crabs, etc.) in any form. They are not fit for consumption in any amount. Ideally, meat/fish would be eaten three (3) times a week or less.

There are plenty of delicious vegetarian dishes you can cook to make improving your man's diet easier. For instance: Vegetarian spaghetti, veggie lasagna, pasta shells stuffed with spinach and ricotta cheese, veggie chili, bean burgers, veggie burgers, plantains with peas and rice, stir fry veggies, vegetable curry, veggie burritos, falafel, etc. The list is endless. Remember; let him eat meat a few times a week unless he decides to give it up. Don't create chaos in the home by trying to force this on him. If you do, he will probably rebel and eat worse just to spite you. Women must realize that we are the doctors in our homes, but the patients are free to make the final choice in their treatment. As long as it does not go against the spiritual foundation of your home, men must feel free. If you decide to go 100% vegetarian/vegan that's great, just don't disturb his peace. Stress is as much of a killer as diet is.

The best approach to get your man on board may be to not even discuss improving his diet. Just start (gradually) making more and more meatless meals. If they are good enough he might not even notice. By not discussing it he has less chance to put up a fight. If he complains then give him some (organic) meat for a few weeks, then (more slowly) start reducing it again. This may take time and many repeated attempts. If he likes your food but asks why there is no meat, you might be safe discussing this with him. You could even show him a documentary on the subject first. Afterward ask his thoughts about it. He may decide to try eating better on his own, he might not.

Never try to force a man to eat something he doesn't like. Don't make strange, unfamiliar foods like tofu kabobs with seaweed marinade. I wouldn't even eat that. Stick with things he likes and you won't get so much resistance.

Pressed for Time

It doesn't have to take a long time to cook meals, especially if you aren't preparing meat. Vegetable dishes can often be made in 10-30 minutes. One trick is to chop up your vegetables as soon as you get home from the grocery store. Then when you are ready to cook, you can just grab whatever you need. If you do this, you can make a stir fry in about 7 minutes or so. It can't get easier than that.

You can also use something called a crock pot, which is also known as a Dutch oven or a slow cooker. These devices cook slowly at very low temperatures. This means you can throw some things in the pot, turn it on low, and dinner will be ready for you in 8-10 hours when you return home. If you are a meat eater, a crock pot will make the most tender meat you have ever tasted. You can use crock pots for vegetarian casseroles as well.

Another helpful contraption is a pressure cooker. They cut cooking time significantly. If you are on the go, this is a worthwhile purchase.

Women love to use time as an excuse because it sounds legitimate. Honestly, I can make rice pilaf in 10 minutes. Rice-a-Roni usually takes about 20 minutes. I can make a pizza in 15-20 minutes. It usually takes 30-45 minutes to have one delivered. I can fry fish in 8-10 minutes. By the time I sit in line at a takeout joint and then drive home, my guests could have been finished eating if I had made it myself. We have to stop lying to ourselves. It doesn't have to take hours to cook a decent meal for your family. It does take love, care and planning.

Making Men's Night Healthy

Men really appreciate it when their woman cooks, especially if they aren't expecting a meal. This is a great opportunity to nourish him. Generally speaking, as long as food looks good and tastes good, your man will at least give it a try. Next time your man has friends over to watch a movie or sports event, try surprising them with healthy vegetarian 7 layer nachos. Not only will this make you the most popular wife in the world, it will give them added nutrition instead of a bunch of junk. These nachos are easy to construct, but remember that presentation is everything, so make it pretty.

Layer 1: *Tortilla chips. You can use plain, seasoned or colored chips. I prefer spicy "Red Hot Blues" which are available in health food stores.*

Layer 2: *Sauté multi-colored bell peppers, chili peppers and onions in olive oil. Season them with sea salt and Ms. Dash garlic and herb while cooking. Cook until they are tender- but not soggy or sloppy looking.*

Layer 3: *Corn. If you can find fire-roasted corn that will be even better! Just heat it up in a pan with a bit of butter, sea salt and Mrs. Dash garlic and herb seasoning.*

Layer 4: *Salsa.*

Layer 5: *Seasoned black beans. If using canned beans, drain most of the liquid out. Warm on low heat with a variety of spices such as sea salt, cumin, garlic, chili powder, chipotle powder, onion powder and even a pinch of cinnamon works well. Make them to suit your taste preferences.*

Layer 6: *Sour Cream (organic) placed on top of the beans.*

Layer 7: *Cheese of your choice (organic) sprinkled on top. Cheddar, Pepper Jack and Spanish cheeses work well.*

Optional: add bottled jalapeno rings or olive slices

Put it all together and you have a great, but healthy snack for the menfolk to enjoy. I generally start with beans in the middle and nachos surrounding them, then layer everything else on top. Beans are hearty, and you need plenty of tortillas to pick up the filling, so that is the best way to arrange it. You can also make individual portions so you don't have to worry about "double dips".

Now just because you cooked for them doesn't mean they want you hanging around. Serve the tortillas, fill up their cups and leave them to do whatever it is that men do when we aren't around.

Kitchen Tips:

- Always wash off lids before you open cans. You can't imagine the nastiness that they are exposed to in factories and warehouses (dust, animal feces, dirty hands, etc.) If you don't wash the top of the can before opening it, inevitably the germs on the lid get in contact with the liquid in the cans. It's not sanitary.

- Lemon juice removes stubborn onion odors from Tupperware. Just pour a little lemon juice in the container and fill it with water. Let it sit for a few minutes. Repeat if necessary. Your containers will be as good as new.
- Use a few drops of pure lemon essential oil to sterilize your kitchen every day. Just put a few drops on a damp rag or paper towel and wipe the counters (and appliances). This makes the kitchen smell fresh and disinfects it- without unhealthy chemicals. Go a little heavier on the Lemon oil if you have prepared meat on the counters. American non-organic meat is packed with fecal contamination.
- Everyone should have a small herb garden in their kitchen. Herb gardens are not only an introduction into caring for plants, they are great for cooking! Fresh herbs can be expensive. Try growing Basil, Rosemary, Thyme, Mint, Oregano, Lemon Balm, or anything that you use on a regular basis. Having an aloe plant in the home should be mandatory. It helps heal minor burns and is also a source of nutrition.
- Be careful when you are decorating your kitchen and dining room. The colors you choose can either suppress or stimulate the appetite. Appetite stimulating colors include: red, orange, turquoise and yellow. Appetite suppressing colors include: dark blue, gray, purple and black. If you are dieting, use these suppressing colors in plates, place mats and other decor. Otherwise, use the stimulating colors.
- Need to know if an egg is fresh? Drop it in 6 inches of water. If it sinks, it's fresh. If it remains submerged but the widest end points up, it's older but still okay. If it floats, its old- you might want to buy some new eggs.
- If you add too much salt in something while it's still cooking, throw in a peeled potato. The potato will absorb some of the salt. Discard the potato afterward.
- If you add too much of a hot spice like Cayenne, try adding a little milk, cream or other dairy product to balance it out. I'm not sure why it works, but it does.
- Freeze fruit juices and nectars instead of water for use as ice cubes. This adds flavor to drinks instead of watering them down. Mango ice cubes (made from mango nectar) melted in lemonade is very good.

- Mrs. Dash is a healthy brand of seasoning blends with plenty of flavors to choose from. It contains no salt or MSG, so use as much as you like. Many times you can find the same flavors in store brands priced much cheaper. Just read the label to be sure there is no salt in the store brand.
- If you must eat meat, ALWAYS buy organic, grass fed or Amish raised. Never buy cheap meat. Most meat on the American market is not fit to be consumed.
- White whole wheat flour tastes milder than regular (red) whole wheat, but still gives you superior nutrition.
- Sea salt is a much healthier choice than regular white salt. Try to purchase sea salt crystals and grind them yourself. My preference is Himalayan pink sea salt crystals.
- Always buy organic dairy products and eggs or you risk ingesting hormones and chemicals. Organic dairy isn't perfect, but it's a million times better!
- Wheat flour is not the same as 100% whole wheat flour. It must say 100% Whole Wheat Flour.
- Soy is not a miracle food. It is hard to digest and acts as an estrogen. Don't make a habit of using soy to replace meat.
- Artificial sweeteners are worse than sugar. Never opt for sugar free commercial products made with aspartame, NutraSweet, Equal, etc. Stevia is okay as a sugar replacement if you like how it tastes.
- Applesauce is a great replacement for oil in baked goods. Feel free to substitute an equal amount of applesauce to replace vegetable oil.
- Hummus is a good, nutritious replacement for mayonnaise. It is made from chick peas (garbanzo beans). Hummus also makes a great dipping sauce for chips and veggies.

Simple Recipes:

Navy Bean Vegetable Soup

Ingredients:

2 cups dry navy beans

1 large onion

1-2 medium bell peppers

3-4 stalks of celery

2-3 carrots

1 14 oz. can of diced tomatoes (Drain them well! The liquid will make the soup bitter.)

1 tbsp. sage

1 tbsp. turmeric (Caution: turmeric is a dye. It stains!)

1 tbsp. cane sugar

2-3 cloves garlic (minced)

1 bay leaf (optional)

2-3 tbsp. butter

Sea salt (to taste)

Cayenne pepper (to taste)

Directions:

Begin by soaking the beans the night before. This will lessen the cooking time. The next day, rinse the beans well. Rubbing the beans together as they are being washed helps remove some of the grime and excess starch. Pick through the beans and discard any oddly colored or wrinkled beans. Also discard any stones that may be mixed in.

Place the beans in a large pot. Add water. The water should reach about 3-4 inches above the beans. Allow the beans to cook until they become tender. This will take anywhere from one hour to several hours depending on the level of heat that you use. Add more water if needed to prevent the beans from burning. As it cooks, when you see foam bubbling on the top, scoop it off with a spoon. This helps lessen gas. Once the beans are tender, add the vegetables, butter and spices. If you were cooking the beans on high heat, reduce it to medium/low. Continue to cook until the beans are extremely tender, and the vegetables are tender. The broth should become slightly thick. Some people prefer to blend the soup at this point to make it smooth. I choose to serve it as-is. Remember to remove the Bay leaf before serving.

*Soup tastes even better the next day

Hot Cauliflower Bites

Ingredients:

1 head of cauliflower (chopped into bite-sized pieces)

1 ½ cups of flour

1 ¾ cups veggie or chicken broth

1 tbsp. garlic powder

1 tbsp. onion powder

Dash of sea salt

1 cup of hot sauce

1 tbsp. butter (melted)

Directions:

Preheat the oven to 450°F. Lightly grease a cookie sheet.

Combine the broth, flour, and spices in a bowl and stir until it forms a batter. Coat the individual cauliflower pieces with the batter, a few at a time. Shake off any excess batter and place the cauliflower on a lightly greased cookie sheet. Bake it for 15-20 minutes until golden brown. Feel free to flip the pieces over to prevent burning, if needed. In the meantime, mix the hot sauce with the butter. In a large bowl, toss the baked cauliflower with the sauce. Place it back on the cookie sheet. Bake for an additional 3-5 minutes or until crisp, and then drizzle with any excess sauce.

This is a decent alternative for hot wings. It doesn't "taste like chicken" but it gives a lot of "hot wing" flavor. Feel free to serve with celery and blue cheese or ranch dressing (organic).

*For MILD flavored sauce: Mix ½ cup teriyaki sauce with ½ cup sweet chili sauce, 1 tbsp. of brown sugar and a dash of ginger, garlic and smoked paprika.

Roasted Mushrooms

Ingredients:

3 tbsp. sunflower oil

1 lemon (organic)

1 tsp. dried rosemary (fine, young springs not the old hard ones)

5 cups mixed mushrooms (your choice: white, baby bellas, porcini, etc.)

¼ cup grated parmesan and romano cheese blend

Sprinkle of salt

Sprinkle of smoked cayenne or chipotle powder

Directions:

Preheat oven to 400 degrees.

Chop the mushrooms in half (small mushrooms can be left whole if desired) and place them in a large bowl. Zest the lemon. In a small bowl mix the oil, lemon zest and rosemary. Cover the mushrooms with the oil mixture. Sprinkle the mushrooms with salt and cayenne/chipotle pepper. Place on a pan in a single layer. Allow this to bake 10-15 minutes depending on the size of the mushrooms. Remove from the oven, stir and add the cheese. Return the mushrooms to the oven for another 5-7 minutes or until they are done. Remove from the oven, cover with a splash of lemon juice and stir. Serve.

*These mushrooms work well as a topping for angel hair pasta with a garlic alfredo sauce. They can also be used as a vegetarian side dish or a filling for a wrap or Panini sandwich.

Herb Roasted Salmon

Ingredients:

6 tbsp. olive oil

2 cloves garlic (chopped finely)

1 tsp. dried basil

¾-1 tsp. kosher salt (to taste)

1 tsp. pepper

1 tbsp. fresh chopped parsley

1 tbsp. old bay seasoning

2-3 salmon fillets

Directions:

Stir all ingredients except the fillets together into a marinade. Add the fillets, making sure to coat all sides well with the marinade. Let the fish marinate 12-24 hours in the refrigerator, the longer the better.

Wrap the individual fillets, smothered in the marinade, in aluminum foil. Place the individually wrapped fillets in a cake pan to prevent any oil from leaking in the oven. Cook on 375F for 25-35 minutes depending on the thickness of the fillets. It is done when the salmon is opaque throughout.

Cajun Alfredo Sauce

Ingredients:

1 cup grated organic parmesan/romano cheese mix

1 cup organic milk (more if needed)

2 tbsp. organic butter

1 tsp. garlic powder

1 tsp. onion powder

1 tsp. Italian herb

1 tsp. chipotle pepper powder

1 tsp. smoked paprika

Sea salt (to taste)

Smoke seasoning (optional)

Directions:

Wisk all of the ingredients in a pot over medium heat until the cheese is melted. You can use additional milk to thin it out if needed. Serve with al dente pasta, veggies or chicken.

Spinach Croquettes

Ingredients:

1 12oz bag of chopped spinach (thawed)

1 egg

½ small onion (diced, optional)

¼ cup shredded or small cubes of cheddar cheese

¼ cup cheese flavored crackers (crushed finely)

¼ tsp. chipotle pepper

Sea salt (to taste)

1 tsp. garlic powder

1 tsp. Mrs. Dash garlic & herb

Seasoned flour (as needed)

Oil of your choice (for sautéing)

Directions:

Squeeze out as much excess water as possible from the thawed spinach. Heat some oil in a pan and sauté the onion until soft. After the onion is cooked, place all ingredients except the flour and oil in a large bowl. Mix well.

Pour a little flour out and add the same seasonings you put in the spinach- or whatever other seasonings you prefer. Season the flour generously, and then mix well. I like to do this on aluminum foil or wax paper so that I can easily dispose of the remaining flour afterwards. Form the spinach mixture into patties and dip both sides in flour. Sauté the croquettes in the oil until the first sides are brown (about 5 minutes). Flip and allow the other side to brown and get crisp. Place on a foil lined cookie sheet and bake at 350 for 10-15 minutes until heated throughout. Serve.

Banana Mini Pancakes (no flour, no sugar)

Ingredients:

4 eggs

2 ripe bananas

1 tsp. pure vanilla extract

A pinch of salt

Cinnamon and ginger (optional, to taste)

Butter or coconut oil for frying

Directions:

Mix together eggs, bananas and spices in a blender or food processor. Cut the heat on medium/low. Melt a little butter or coconut oil in a non-stick skillet or griddle. Scoop the batter into the skillet using a ¼ cup measuring cup to form small "pancakes". Slowly cook until golden brown on one side, then flip. When the second side is brown, remove from heat and place the pancakes on a plate. Serve with butter and pure maple syrup or honey.

*These pancakes are very sweet, but feel free to add chocolate chips if you'd like.

Apple Spice Oatmeal (No added Sugar)

Ingredients:

3 1/3 cups apple juice

1 medium-large apple (peeled and diced)

1 tsp. (or more) apple pie spice or cinnamon

1 tbsp. (or more) honey or pure maple syrup (not pancake syrup)

1 tsp. pure vanilla extract

1 1/3 cups quick cooking oatmeal

½ tsp. salt

Directions:

Start by heating the apple juice in a pot over a medium flame. While that is heating up, dice the apples and add them to the juice along with the apple pie spice, honey/maple syrup and vanilla extract. Allow it to cook until apples begin to soften (but don't let them get mushy). After the apples are no longer raw, add the oatmeal and salt. Cook until thickened. Cover and let sit for a few minutes.

*You can also add raisins, butter or brown sugar depending on your preference. This makes about 3 servings.

Sunrise Muffins

Ingredients:

3 eggs

1 cup applesauce

1 cup cane sugar

1 cup light brown sugar

4 cups grated carrots

1 tbsp. pure vanilla extract

2 cups all-purpose flour

1 cup white whole wheat flour

1 tbsp. ground cinnamon

1 tbsp. ground ginger

1 tsp. baking soda

¼ tsp. baking powder

1 tsp. sea salt

½ cup purple raisins

¾ cups golden raisins

Directions:

Preheat the oven to 325F. Lightly grease muffin pans.

In a large bowl, beat eggs until they become frothy. Mix in the applesauce, brown sugar and cane sugar. Add in the vanilla and carrots. Combine flour, cinnamon, ginger, baking soda, baking powder, salt and all the raisins in a separate bowl. Slowly add the dry ingredients into the wet ingredients. Mix until the batter is combined, but do not over mix! Stop stirring as soon as the batter comes together. Pour batter into muffin pans and bake 16-20 minutes or until done.

No-Bake Lime Cheesepie (No Sugar Added)

Ingredients:

1 8oz pkg. cream cheese (organic)

1 14oz can of sweetened condensed milk (organic)

1 tbsp. Vanilla extract (vanilla beans can be used)

½ cup of fresh squeezed lime juice

1 graham cracker crust

Directions:

Blend together cream cheese and condensed milk. Stir in the vanilla and lime juice. Mix well. Pour the mixture into the pie crust. Chill until thickened to the desired consistency. It will thicken as it sets. Garnish and serve.

Creamy Ginger Drink

Ingredients:

1 ginger tea bag

1 ½ cups of organic milk

1 ½ cups of water

Organic cane sugar (to taste)

Directions:

Heat the milk and water in a small pot over medium heat. Add the ginger tea bag and allow it to steep for 10-15 minutes. Sweeten as desired.

For more recipes visit: ***www.message2theblackfam.com***

In closing, mature men with good sense want a domestically capable woman. They want to be able to enjoy a clean home and good food. They want well behaved, respectful children. They want an elegant wife. Does that mean that only you who should be in the kitchen all day? Not necessarily. It depends on work schedules, ability, etc. Every relationship is different. But you should know how! Just like he should know basic home and auto repair, as well as self-defense! Food is medicine. Food is an aphrodisiac. Food maintains life. Get comfortable in the kitchen.

Chapter Six: Sensual Healing

Sexual ability comes naturally. So-called experts try to make sex seem complicated in order to make you feel inadequate. They do this to sell their books and teaching aids. The porn industry doesn't help much either. Watching explicit movies slowly desensitizes you to the inherent pleasures of joining together with your man. As you watch others engaging in cheap, misogynistic sex, your excitement level dulls and you begin to seek more and more extreme and/or unnatural actions to keep sex fresh. Men who learn by watching porn are also inclined to believe that women enjoy certain acts that we do not. It's a male-based fantasy world. I suggest going back to the basics - a man and woman uniting in respect and love.

It's important to start from scratch with a normal, sane sexual routine because the type of sex that has been presented to us is designed to block the normal bonding that should take place during lovemaking. Slow things down. Stay in the moment and focus on what is taking place. Look in your man's eyes. Whisper softly in his ear. Kiss his neck. Run your hands over his body. Do all the loving things that the media skips over in smutty productions. These small things are what create intimacy and should be the rule - not the exception.

Sex should be a beautiful experience between a man and woman. Our creator designed our bodies to have sex. There is nothing to be ashamed of, unless you begin to venture into perversity. Contrary to what the "experts" claim, the secret to good sex is not being a gymnast, a contortionist or a stripper. The secret to a satisfying sexual relationship is being in love and feeling secure and comfortable. When you make love to someone you have deep feelings for, your body's reactions become more sensitive. Experiencing these heightened sensations, along with knowing and trusting your man, makes sex far more pleasurable than a random encounter would be. The "7 Year Itch" does not need to occur in your marriage.

There is nothing wrong with researching and enhancing healthy sexual relations. It is a great idea to get a modern adaptation of the Kama Sutra, authentic Tantra (avoid any aspects that are objectionable) or erotic massage books. I will give you a few other pointers as we proceed. Keeping things fresh and interesting is vital, but this should be done wholesomely. Most importantly, relax and enjoy yourself.

Communicating

If you expect to be satisfied in a relationship, you must be tactfully honest. This means that you don't fake orgasms, but you don't insult his abilities either. The male ego is sensitive! It cannot stand direct negative critiques. It is important to be indirect and subtle. You never tell a man outright that he is not pleasing you. Instead you teach him what you enjoy. Every person is different. What worked on the last person might not work on you. Different strokes for different folks (no pun intended). That doesn't make him a bad lover; it just means you can have a lot of fun exploring each other to see what works for you!

Understanding men is important. Men rebel against unsolicited feminine advice almost automatically. They also get extremely defensive which can lead to many unnecessary problems. The best way to win a man over to your way of thinking is to make him think it was his idea in the first place. This is part of "righteous deception" and is a very handy skill to have. It also gives you something to laugh at when you hear him declaring "his new idea". On the other hand, if you are aggressive, belligerent or insulting, you can forget it. No one responds well to that foolishness. Your man is your life partner, not your sparring partner. You should be his support.

Never, ever, ever compare your man to an ex sexually or in any other way. This is one of the most damaging and least intelligent things you could possibly do. If your man feels you prefer sex with another man, or that another man is even crossing your mind, you are going to have problems. No man who cares about you wants to think about you having sex with someone else. Comparing your husband to an ex, especially about sex, makes you lose a lot of respectability in his eyes, knocks you off your pedestal and builds a deep insecurity and resentment of you that he may never get over. Don't do it. This will NOT make him want to do better. It may make him purposely perform worse (retaliation or apathy), cheat (to prove he can satisfy a woman) or leave (since he can't satisfy you anyway).

How do you teach him tactfully? As I said, NEVER fake satisfaction. This is counterproductive because it allows him to continue doing the wrong things. Instead, when he does something you like, be vocal.

When he does something that doesn't work for you, be silent. **If you experience discomfort or pain, speak up!** Usually a man will notice if you are vocal then become silent. Generally he will ask you if there is a problem or if you are enjoying yourself. Take that opportunity to communicate. You don't have to outright say you don't like his performance. It is gentler to say, "It feels even better when you..." or "I'd love to try it like this...." Chances are he will listen and make adjustments. The beauty of this technique is it allows his ego to make him believe he discovered how to please you on his own. This boosts his confidence in his ability which is always beneficial. Remember, you are a wise and feminine woman. Protect the male ego with tact at all cost.

> <u>Helpful Hint:</u> *If you just sit around complaining about not being satisfied without doing anything to improve your condition, you are being lazy. If you are lazy, he might not be pleased with your performance either. Maybe he's just too nice to express it. If you don't like how he's making love to you, try making love to him, as well as utilizing the strategies stated above.*

Exercise

One of the best things you can do to enjoy an exciting sex life with your man is to get in shape! Not only does this make you look great, it also gives you confidence. Confidence is very attractive. Most men get very annoyed by insecure women who are afraid to show their bodies, only want to have sex in the dark or only have sex in positions they think are flattering to their perceived flaws. Some men cheat for this very reason. Men are visual. They want to be able to freely admire the beauty of their spouse. Instead of being ashamed of your body, fix the problems! Most Black men don't even notice what we consider flaws anyway, so if you are in reasonably good shape, he will love what he sees.

Developing good muscle tone allows you to improve your stamina in various positions. You don't want to have to switch up when things are getting good. I would suggest doing several sets of squats daily to strengthen your quadriceps. This helps quite a bit with "female superior" (woman on top) positions. Weak quads limit your ability.

Pushups strengthen your arms which allow stability when you need to be able to hold up your body weight. Bellydance teaches how to isolate and loosen your muscles. Muscle control is very important because the ability to loosen and tighten muscles allows you to create and control climax. Pilates increases flexibility which promotes creativity and fun. There is nothing worse than having sex interrupted because someone got a cramp or a charlie-horse (though it can be very funny). Sex is not meant for lazy people. There is nothing worse than lying around uninvolved. Physical fitness increases your overall health and energy level which is vital for great sex.

As you tone different muscle groups, you can't forget about your PC muscles and the surrounding muscles of the genital area. These muscles allow you to tighten your grip, reach orgasm easier, and even enable your vaginal muscles to massage the male organ internally during intercourse. You can begin practicing by stopping the flow of urine when using the bathroom. This will show you some of the specific muscles you need to target. Do several reps throughout the day. No one will be able to tell what you are doing, so you can feel free to do this anytime, anyplace. As you become more skilled you will be able to isolate different muscle groups in the groin, increasing your control. You can find vaginal weights and jade eggs that also work to tone these muscles. Under normal circumstances they are not necessary, though they may help after child birth or other trauma. For further study, research Kegel exercises.

Toys and Aides

By toning your genital muscles, you should not feel the need to rely on weird sex toys such as vibrators. Vibrators, though effective, are extremely unnatural. There is a natural vibration and energy exchange that occurs when a man and woman join together. There are extreme healing powers in healthy, committed, heterosexual unions that cannot be duplicated with machinery. You may have heard of women having sex that was so good it made them cry. This is a form of real life sexual healing. The connection gained through a deeply loving sexual union allows you to let go of past emotional and sexual traumas. Vibrators are made by an unnatural, freakish race of people and do not promote emotional health in Black women.

Vibrators were originally created to relieve white females of a condition called "Hysteria" or "Female Hysteria". Hysteria occurred because of the white male's sexual inadequacies. He was not able and/or interested in pleasing his spouse; therefore, she often suffered emotional issues like nervousness, insomnia and irritability among other symptoms due to prolonged sexual dissatisfaction. For a long time upper-class white women would go to their physicians for manual genital massages to "cure" this condition with orgasm. Vibrators were invented to save time, making treatment quick and easy. Truth is stranger than fiction.

Black men are well able to satisfy their spouses. They are gifted spiritually, emotionally and physically to be able to relate to us like no other can. Their sweet soulfulness soothes, comforts, excites and stimulates us effortlessly. This is why I am amazed at the amount of men who encourage their women to use vibrators, sometimes even in bed while they are present. Ladies, you are making your man lazy by doing this. He will not take the time to explore your body, your likes and your desires if he can just "flip a switch". Allow him to learn how to touch you and use his body to achieve the same results.

Often Black women are left unfulfilled and feeling empty after using these gadgets because Black women are divinely designed to relate to our complement (a Black man). She draws energy from her man every time he enters her. This is why the man is often worn out after a sexual encounter while the woman may be energized. The woman is built to receive both physically and mentally. That explains why women sometimes look sloppy, act agitated or become impossible to deal with when they are involuntarily celibate for too long. The energy received from male penetration balances the female and is an absolute necessity. This is one reason I never suggest using sex as a weapon. In the long-run, it will hurt you just as much as your man.

There are also health dangers due to the chemicals used in the cheap plastics used to make these devices, especially the ones that are inserted. Phthalates are a major concern with some sex toys. These chemical have been linked to birth defects and may increase the absorption of other toxic chemicals. Phthalates are used often in soft, jelly-like plastic toys. Generally speaking, the harder vibrators/dildos are made from silicone which is supposedly safer. I'm skeptical. Remember, your skin is porous. That means that any chemicals that you put on your skin or in your vagina can be absorbed.

Another issue with harsh vibrators is the temporary loss of sensation. Using sex toys too often can cause the clitoris to gradually become numb which makes it harder and harder to reach clitoral orgasm. This may also occur with "clit piercings". This is a reversible condition. You can either stop using the vibrator for a period of time or take out the "clit ring" for a period of time to allow normal sensation to return. Either way, why bother? Loss of clitoral feeling is not cute or desirable. Sometimes we do way too much in the quest for satisfaction.

Other sexual aides such as lotions, oils, edible products, tightening creams and lubricants often contain questionable or downright nasty ingredients. Number one on the list is urea which is basically urine. This chemical is in many edible and non-edible products. There may also be gelatin or glycerin which may be made from pork (check with the manufacture to be sure). There could also be cancer causing dyes, artificial flavors, fragrance, etc. Use extreme caution when shopping for these products. If you need an alternative lubricant or massage oil, try coconut oil. It has anti-bacterial properties and is natural.

Sex as a Weapon

Helpful Hint: Remember, using sex as a weapon is a horrible idea. The desire to use sex as a weapon says a lot about you and your relationship. Women use sex as a weapon for many reasons. None of them are good or productive.

Some women use sex as a weapon because their men won't submit to them or cater to their frivolous needs. This is completely immature and petty. Thinking like this shows a lack of femininity and an abundance of arrogance. A man is not supposed to submit to your whims. You are supposed to submit to him. It is a man's duty to provide basic necessities for you (food, clothing, shelter). It is not his job to spoil you, buy every silly trinket you want or kiss your feet. He wouldn't be a man worthy of respect if he constantly did that.

Other women use sex as a weapon because their feelings were hurt. This is also immature. If you intend to have a relationship with longevity, you must communicate. If he was insensitive, discuss it rationally. If he disappoints you, tell him (tactfully). If he was disrespectful or careless, talk about it! Using sex as a weapon instead of talking it out is one good way to kill your relationship. You do nothing but build resentment which is like kryptonite to a marriage.

Sex is unifying. It brings you together using all of your senses. You are forced to see, smell, touch, taste and hear each other up close and personal. This is often the best way to smooth over difficulties and stay connected (make up sex). When you decide to abandon the physical side of your relationship over petty disagreements and misunderstandings, you are allowing a wedge to grow between you. This is a very dangerous gamble to take. Over time this can wear down the connection, extinguish the fire of attraction and ultimately lead to looking for relief outside of the relationship.

I am a firm believer that you should not attempt to hold your partner "hostage" in marriage in any way. This means: thinking it is okay to "let yourself go", gaining an inordinate amount of weight, regularly refusing sexual advancements, or not doing your part in any other way. Many of us do this thinking that we can get away with it because "they are stuck with us". I'll let you in on a little secret. No one in this society is stuck with anyone else. Please don't find out the hard way that relationships can, and do end when one person gets tired of this type of foolishness.

Hygiene

<u>Helpful Hint:</u> Cleanliness is next to Godliness. You must NEVER overlook this aspect of lovemaking. There is nothing worse than being near a woman who smells like fish instead of flowers. It is very offensive and can make you lose respect for that woman. Bad body odors are very unladylike.

Refined women bathe often. Washing once a day is mandatory. Twice a day (more if it is hot) is ideal. You should take a bath to freshen up when you rise, and again at the end of the day. Be sure to keep your breath fresh. You can add a drop of pure mint, clove or cinnamon essential oil on your toothbrush along with toothpaste when brushing for extra freshness. These oils taste very strong so please don't use more than 1 drop.

Never get into bed dirty, funky or sweaty. Sheets should be changed at least once a week or anytime you have sex, whichever is more frequent. When you wash your sheets it is good to sprinkle a little baking powder and essential oil, such as lavender, on your mattress. This helps clean and freshen the mattress. You can wipe or vacuum off any excess. Your bed should be a sacred space. Take care of it and keep it pretty and made up when you aren't in it.

You should not allow your man to touch your intimate areas with dirty hands. This increases the chance of infections and is just nasty in general. Your vagina is very sensitive and should only be approached with respect and cleanliness. If he has not washed his hands, if his fingernails are dirty or if he touches something germy, be sure to have him freshen up. Do this in a feminine way and assure him the reward will be worth the effort. Sooner or later hand washing will become habitual for him and a small price to pay for access to you. Be sure that you wash your hands as well before coming close to your vagina (using the restroom or tending to menstrual issues). Your womb must be protected.

Using commercialized chemical douches should not be a necessary part of your routine. The vagina cleans itself sufficiently under normal circumstances. If you maintain a high standard of hygiene and you still suffer from odors, you may need to change your diet. Meat is very constipating. As it sits in your intestines it putrefies, creating some of the most horrible odors known to man. Start eating high fiber foods, especially fruits. Fruits help to normalize your elimination, and also help to sweeten your smell. Pineapple works especially well for men and women. Start limiting your meat intake. You should not eat meat every day of the week. Experiment with different meatless options sometimes. It is important to allow your digestive system to function properly.

It is a good idea to let your vagina breathe. It is not always necessary to wear panties around the house. As a matter of fact, if you have a window facing a private area you may choose to discretely expose your vagina to the Sun's purifying rays from time to time. You can wear a loose skirt and lay on the floor in front of a high window so that no perverts can sneak a peek. Wear skirts whenever possible; they are much better than pants for air circulation.

If none of this helps, you might want to visit a doctor to be sure you don't have any STD's or infections.

Anal sex is a filthy habit that many Black people have picked up in the last decade or so. In my younger days the topic of anal sex among Black people was completely taboo. Unfortunately, today's youth are frequently practicing this filthy deviant act. Even extremely religious girls are engaging in anal penetration because they believe that anal sex does not negate their virginity. Not only is this repulsive from a sanitary point of view, it can be extremely harmful to your body. The muscles of rectum are only designed to allow feces to be released. Unlike the vagina, the anus is delicate and can be easily damaged by forcing a penis (or other objects) into it. It is not uncommon for people who have allowed their body to be violated in this way for long periods of time to end up needing diapers when their rectal muscles weaken. You should firmly question the motives of any man who desires to perform sexual acts that are this closely tied to homosexual misbehavior.

Intimate Encounters

Men don't always require sensual lovemaking sessions the way many women do. In fact, it seems that for them sex is a primal desire needed for physical health just like eating, drinking and sleeping. A simple release is often all that is needed to relieve tension and keep them happy. There is nothing wrong with that, especially when pressed for time in today's busy world. "Quickies" can actually work to your advantage during times when you don't really feel like being bothered although you know he needs relief. Genital massage is another option.

However, never be fooled into thinking that men don't enjoy sensual experiences. More specifically, most men like the thought of you going out of your way to pamper and spoil him. Make him feel like a king. There is nothing more attractive than the contrast between feminine and masculine energy. The more feminine you are around him, the more masculine he will become. Men do not like to feel that they are the only ones initiating sex in a relationship. It is fine to be assertive or take the lead during sex, but don't lose your femininity while doing so. Only homosexual males want to be in the bed with someone as masculine as them. Stay soft.

Seduction plays an enormous role in keeping the spark alive in a marriage. Just because you have been with someone for a decade or more doesn't mean that things are destined to become boring. The trick is staying involved and interested in each other and never taking your relationship for granted. Once you become lazy, sex becomes boring and mechanical. Your man relies on you to keep doing the things you did at the beginning of the relationship, and more. As your inhibitions fade away the potential for excitement should grow.

You should find a good time and place for your intimate sessions. It shouldn't always be a last minute romp in the bed before you fall asleep. Put the children to bed early. Find a new location. Ask your man about his fantasies and desires. Switch things up a little. Try a little spontaneity such as:

- If he is a work-a-holic who spends way too much time away from home, send him provocative text messages. Begin a few minutes after he leaves the house and continue every few hours throughout the day. Tell him what you plan to do to him when he gets home. This gives him ample time to prepare as well as an opportunity to savor the thought.
- Surprise him one morning with breakfast in bed. It doesn't have to be a five course meal, but be sure to include aphrodisiac foods. Bring the meal into the bedroom on a tray. You can place a single flower in a vase on the tray for effect. Be sure to serve a beverage such as sparkling white grape juice or orange juice in a nice Champaign glass. Another good idea is to serve strawberries with either whipped cream or chocolate sauce. Tease him while feeding him the berries. Let the fun begin!
- Mark off a day on your calendar at least once a month to have a "date night". Send the children to their grandparents. Get dressed nicely and go out. Spend the night in a hotel if you want a change of scenery.
- Talk to your spouse about your favorite sexual encounter (with him, not someone else!!!!) This will bring back memories and old feelings. Tell him what you liked most about his performance, the atmosphere, etc. If you are descriptive

- enough it will probably awaken the desire in him pretty quickly.
- Sneak into the bathroom while he is taking a shower and get in with him. Wash his back, etc.
- When he gets home from work take off his shoes for him. Later on after he bathes, sit on the floor and give him a foot massage with a nice aphrodisiac essential oil blend. Study acupressure. There are points on the feet that relate directly to the male organ. You can arouse him and he'll be completely unaware of your plot.
- Use the time of your cycle to focus your energy on him. Many couples tend to withdraw from each other during this time instead of making the most of it. Just because penetration may not be on the menu doesn't mean that you can't touch and cater to him, or vice versa. Use every situation to your advantage.
- Next time he irks you, start a pillow fight or play wrestle and allow it to lead to whatever. It beats arguing!
- Choose a good time to make love to him in his sleep. This not violation per se. This is a nice way to say "Good morning!"

Candlelight is great. Not only does it appeal to his visual nature, that type of lighting is usually very flattering. Good lighting is great for boosting confidence. Scented candles make the air sweet in addition to supplying light. This helps make the environment more sensual. Himalayan Salt Lamps provide a soft glow similar to candle light. These lamps also cleanse the air. While having mirrors in the bedroom is considered bad feng shui, it can really liven up your love life. Again, men are visual. Almost any way that you can cater to his need to see and watch is worth trying. Have fun! Sex does not need to be too serious.

Never believe that because you may be extraordinarily attractive, you can allow your sexual performance to be weak. This is why some men cheat on beautiful women with others who aren't considered as aesthetically pleasing. We should not follow degenerate European sex standards but that doesn't mean you should lay there staring at the ceiling either. Black men want to know that you are enjoying yourself. They also want you to make an effort. I have already stated this but I feel the need to reiterate. Don't be lazy!

Ejaculation Issues

Just as women lose a lot of nutrients during menstruation, men lose many nutrients during ejaculation. It is important to their health to replace these lost vitamins and minerals. This frequent loss can lead to signs of premature aging such as gray hair. Number one on the replenishment list is Zinc. Zinc is important to male sexual health, especially the prostate gland. It is abundant in sperm and thus lost during intimacy. Zinc can be replaced by taking a natural food based vitamin or by diet. Decent sources of zinc include: crimini mushrooms, shiitake mushrooms, spinach, asparagus, maple syrup, green peas, yogurt, oats, pumpkin seeds, navy beans, sunflower seeds, sesame seeds, and spelt. Try working these into his diet on a regular basis.

Another way to control a severe loss of nutrients is by learning an ancient practice called injaculation. This allows a man to have powerful orgasms without emitting semen by squeezing and controlling his pelvic muscles. The exercises used during injaculation are very similar to the ones mentioned previously for women. This topic is too lengthy to explain in depth here, but there are several books available, as well as free information that can be found via the internet. This also has the benefit of allowing him to have sex for longer periods and reach climax several times. Look into it by googling the keyword "injaculation". Practice makes perfect.

Erectile dysfunction (ED) is affecting an astonishing number of young men. More disturbing is the fact that ED usually indicates bigger issues. I offer many suggestions in chapter 8. The African phallus is a symbol of strength, pride, virility and Black manhood. Don't neglect it by ignoring the warning signs of problems.

Chapter Seven: Nurturing His Children

A quick way to lose the respect of a Black man is to mistreat his children. Black women are getting harsher with our children every day. We are using them to take out our anger and frustration on. They have become burdens instead of "bundles of joy". It is not uncommon to hear women call their children the "n-word", tell them they're stupid or blame them for looking or acting like their father. Mothering skills are at an all-time low in the Black community. We leave our boys and girls with people we don't know well, putting them at risk for molestation. Some of us recklessly, bring unstable men into the home and act surprised when our babies suffer horrific abuse, often leading to death.

Child rearing is another area where our bogus "strong Black woman" attitude, which is really just uncontrolled hostility and immaturity, must change. This is truer if it is directed at a stepchild or children from estranged fathers. These children didn't ask you to bring them into chaotic, unhealthy environments. They deserve to be valued. Never gossip or speak about your man's child negatively to other people. We are supposed to be nurturers. As a matter of fact, you should try even harder with a stepchild so they don't feel like an outcast.

Raising stepchildren can be a very difficult challenge. This is especially true when they were produced through an unwise coupling. Often conception happens before men reach the level of maturity in which they begin to have reasonable standards. Rarely is his "ex" the type of person you would want in your life if you had a choice, yet you are expected to play a role in raising their children. Can you say drama? She may be immature, ignorant, and determined to make everyone's life difficult. She could allow her children to run wild, be disrespectful or unhygienic. The children will most likely look like her, act like her and remind you of her. They may have been told you are the enemy who is stealing their daddy from them. She may make up stories about you. These are all things to carefully consider before you begin the relationship. Once you sign your name on the dotted line it is your duty to deal with the drama, and to do so maturely. Do not take it out on the children. Be an adult.

In my opinion, children are just miniature people. Their stature does not mean they don't deserve respect, attention or love. Some women are not genuinely abusive, but they are guilty of not listening to their children. Many of us talk "at" our children instead of opening up a dialogue with them. Because we seem to have lost interest in our children, we've become out of touch with them. They know you don't understand them. Even worse, you are making no attempt to get to know them. When did our children become such a low priority? As they grow older they begin to respect you less and less, and by the time they reach adolescence they are completely out of control. They will rebel even if they do it out of your sight. Lecturing is not the same as teaching. Communication and courtesy flows both ways.

Girls Need Tenderness & Protection

Female children must be protected at all costs. Little girls are very delicate and can be easily wounded. They need to be safeguarded from physical, sexual and emotional harm. This means you must be careful who you trust around her. She needs a safe, loving place to develop. Predators are lurking everywhere.

Pay attention to everyone who comes into contact with the child including the father, grandparents, aunts and uncles, cousins and family friends. If she doesn't want to be around someone, nonchalantly ask why. You don't want to interrogate, but you do want to make sure everyone is treating her well and no one is trying to violate her in any way. As a parent, you are the first line of defense. Keep your eyes open!

You have to choose your words with sensitivity when speaking to her. Do not let anyone tease her, especially about her looks or intelligence. Silly comments can leave scars that last a lifetime. Many times people tease little girls about skin tone, hair texture and body shape. When they grow up we are repulsed when they go to tanning beds, use bleaching cream, put toxic chemicals on their hair to change its texture and/or color, or develop eating disorders. We never examine how our words affected them. It doesn't matter how beautiful they are, the damage is done.

A good example is Venus and Serena Williams. They were typical looking Black girls while growing up. However, many comedians began making fun of their dark skin and braids as if they were ugly. This happened publicly at a very awkward time in their development. Now we see them as grown adults who are absolutely stunning. Most of us would kill to have a body like theirs. Black men look at them and drool. White women are jealous of them because all the surgery in the world won't allow them reach that level of perfection. However, judging by their actions, dress and presentation, their self-esteem doesn't seem to be as high as it should be. Though we all acknowledge their beauty now, it is obvious they haven't begun to see it themselves.

Another example is Lil' Kim. She was absolutely beautiful when she first came out. She degraded herself, but she was still a very pretty woman. We see as time goes on how much self-hate was lurking beneath the confident facade. All the surgeries on her face and body have completely erased the beautiful gifts she was born with. It's sad to watch, but this is what we do to our young girls.

If the girl is the product of a previous relationship from your husband you must never speak negatively about her mother in her presence. The mother is the closest person to a daughter. Allow the girl to have a positive image of her mother, even if the mother talks about you mercilessly. Be the bigger person. Any decent man wants his baby girl to be cherished and treated like a princess regardless of the circumstances.

Always allow and encourage your man to take his daughters out on "daddy-daughter dates". This can be movies, dinner or a walk in the park. They need this time to bond. It is during these adventures that girls learn how men should treat them (opening doors, paying for dates, etc.). Never stand in the way of a man spending time with his children. Fathers have a special bond with their daughters. If you give him an ultimatum, you will lose 99% of the time. Only a severely insecure person feels threatened by a child.

It is the father's job to teach the daughter about men. He will probably be much more direct with your daughter than you are. This is how men communicate. Don't criticize his method of parenting just because it is different from yours. This contrast creates balance. Learning the nature of her father teaches a little girl how to relate to a man in the future. This is healthy.

<u>Helpful Hint:</u> If you want to keep peace in your relationship, always dress your daughters modestly. Good fathers hate to see little girls, especially their own, dressed provocatively.

Fathers understand the thinking of males much more than we do. It is their job and instinct to protect their women. A short skirt may seem like a simple fashion statement to you, but to a man it might be an invitation to violate and disrespect a female child. Do not allow your daughters to wear miniskirts or shirts that show her belly, breasts or upper arms. This will prevent arguments and encourage self-respect. It is always wise to defer to people who have more knowledge than you. Understand that you will never know as much about men as your spouse does.

Raising a Son Requires You to be Ladylike

Many of the principles taught in this book will help you get along with your male children much better. Because of our history, and sometimes because of our emotional instability as well, Black women tend to be very aggressive with their sons. This always backfires. Sons raised by overly aggressive mothers often grow up having problems with women. They don't respect their mothers because their mothers didn't respect them. This emasculation builds up resentment because the young man's needs are not being met.

Some of us have fallen into this bad habit because of single parenthood. We felt that since we didn't have a man around, we had to be mother and father. Sister, you can never replace his father. Don't waste your time trying. You should concentrate on being a disciplined mother. There is no need to constantly be hollering at your children.

This is very undignified, disrespectful and counterproductive.

You should not hit your children regularly. When you do administer punishment it should be a simple spanking, never punches and slaps made out of anger and frustration. I don't think women know how out of control and savage they look punching their sons in the chest or slapping his face. I wonder if they are going to try that when the child is six feet tall. These behaviors come directly from slavery. We often beat our children to make them behave so "massa" didn't beat them worse. Don't continue in this desperate slave behavior. The best method to get your way with a male of any age is by using tact, respect and being ladylike. This will make him adore you and be more apt to want to please you.

Regardless of age, all males have egos. Even a young boy feels the need to be perceived as big, manly, powerful and competent. You must keep this in mind when relating to them. Just as you stroke your husband's ego, try doing the same with your son. Just as you strive to act more feminine around your man, use femininity with your child. They will respond much better than being yelled at and overpowered. All heterosexual males are drawn to feminine women.

I remember when my stepson was about four years old. He probably weighed about 35 lbs., yet he would go around making everyone feel his non-existent muscles. As you touched his soft little arms he'd exclaim, "I got TOUGH muscles!" I had no idea what a tough muscle was, but to build his little ego I would play along. "You got tough muscles like your daddy!" I'd say while I tried to hold in my laugh. This killed two birds with one stone. Saying those words made the toddler feel manly. It also showed admiration for his father who was usually in the room. His father was made to feel that I was attracted to him and my stepson was encouraged to want to be like his father. Remember, no matter how small the "man" is, charm and ego stroking is always appreciated.

I never had to holler at my stepson. When I was angry "the look" was enough to stop him in his tracks. I never had to spank him. I let his father do that, after a man-to-man conversation. This allowed me to maintain my nurturing role while making my husband the ultimate authority and "bad cop" in the home. When he got out of line I had the luxury of stating, "I can't believe you did so and so. I'm so disappointed. I know that you know better. I'll just have to tell your father." Those words "Tell your father" made the nonsense stop immediately. This only worked because I didn't stand in the way of his father being a man. If I had disrespected him, his son would have lost respect (and fear) for him as well. Always be aware of how your choice of actions will affect your children.

Don't be afraid to say "please" and "thank you" to your sons. Always be kind and respectful to them. Chances are they won't be treated like that elsewhere so make sure he receives it at home daily. He needs to know what dignity and honor feel like. As a he grows into a man he will accept nothing less.

Although it is absolutely necessary to use femininity when rearing sons, it is vital that you don't go to the extreme of babying them. Remember, boys must grow into productive men. Give your male children daily responsibilities and chores. There is nothing worse than a grown man who expects a woman to do everything for him. Helpless males pick up these habits while being spoiled as children. We must develop our sons into young men with a strong character. They should be taught to share, take initiative and work. Always remember, your son is not the man of the house. He's not even a man yet. Let him enjoy his childhood, but teach him what he needs to know to survive as he grows into a husband and father.

I should not need to say this, but unfortunately I must. Never, under any circumstances, should you refer to your son as the n-word. There is no more effective way to communicate hatred and disrespect for a Black person than to do that. You should not use the n-word at all, but certainly not directed at the child you are supposed to nurture. Calling your son the n-word is one of the most devastating things you can do as a parent. I can't stress it enough. Call him your prince, your little king, your seed, or your soldier but never the n-word.

A Good Way to Make Your Man and Child Hate You

Want to lose the respect of two people at once? Just compare the child to their father in a negative way. Here are a few examples:
- You are lazy, just like your father
- You will never amount to anything, just like your father
- You are stupid, just like your father
- I can't stand you. You look just like your father.

- You ain't sh!t, just like your father
- You ain't nothin' but a nappy headed "n-word", just like your father.

Children love to be compared to their parents, but only in good ways. I am always amazed when I see my people saying these things to their children, usually their sons. I wonder if they hear themselves. If you are having problems with your children, do you think ostracizing them and their daddy will help?

Speaking to your children in this way instantly lowers their self-esteem. If momma says you are worthless or stupid, she must be correct! She gave birth to you and she knows you best, right? If momma thinks you are stupid and won't amount to anything, why try?

This also alienates the father who could provide help with guidance and discipline. Since momma says daddy is no good, why should the child listen to him? He's just a no good n-word who doesn't take care of him anyway. On top of that, momma says you are doomed to grow to be just like him.

To a father, especially one who was told these things by his mother, this creates an instant hatred of you. It's hard to gain back any level of respect once you have let these words fly out of your mouth. Check your attitude. Go blow off steam if you need to. Once you say things like this, the damage is done.

Disagreements

Don't argue with your man in front of the children. You must present a united front. Adult business is not for the ears of children. Disagreeing privately has the added benefit of making little ones feel secure. Young children may overhear a simple disagreement between their parents and assume it means they will be filing for a divorce tomorrow. This can be traumatic for sensitive children, especially girls. They know that having an intact family is the exception to the rule in our community. To some children, this really is a concern.

Never disagree about the children in front of the children! Little people are very wise and manipulative, no matter how cute they may look. Don't be fooled. If they see any discord, most of them won't hesitate to divide and conquer. Never doubt their genius or sneakiness when trying to get their way in the household. It is not unheard of for a child to ask the mother if they can go somewhere. If the mother says no, they will go ask the father who is likely to say yes. Then they will go back to the mother and casually mention going there again. When mom says no once more, the child will say, "But my daddy said I could go!" Always communicate together before telling a child yes or no. There should be steep penalties for the child asking one parent for permission after the other gives an answer. Don't let them get away with these games. Show them you are united.

Even if they don't witness disagreements in person, sometimes children will still play one parent against the other to push their agenda. I know of a family where hygiene was very important. One of the stepchildren lived in a different home with her mother where bathing was optional. One hot summer day while visiting at her father's home, the girl's stepmother told her to take a bath before bedtime. The child complained that she had already taken a bath the day before. The stepmother patiently explained, "Young ladies must take baths at least once a day, especially as they reach adolescence. Odors become much stronger as you grow up, especially on hot days when you've been out playing and sweating. It is nasty for women to get in the habit of not keeping themselves clean. That's why I'm teaching you to bathe regularly." The girl, determined not to take a bath, slyly looked at her stepmother unashamed. She said, "So you calling my momma nasty? She don't take a bath every day!" The stepmother wanted to say "Heck yeah, that heifer is nasty if she doesn't bathe!" Instead she told the father to make the girl get in the tub. As you see, these precious little angels can turn into Gremlins in just a few seconds (smile). Never give them ammunition.

Your King (and the Relationship) is Number One

Now that we have that out of the way, I must discuss a controversial reality. Your man is always number one. He comes before your friends, your family, and yes, even those sweet little babies. Many women aren't going to like how that sounds, but it's true.

Realistically, caring for your family is generally a sort of triage. Obviously if your baby falls and hits her head while the father is waiting on you to bring him some chips, he will have to wait a minute until the baby is consoled. We deal with the most severe needs first. No real man would want his children to be neglected. However, all things being equal, he comes first.

Even when things are calm and there in no emergency occurring, we still tend to cater to the children before our spouse. I have even seen women tell their husbands to be quiet so that a child can show her a new toy. In case you didn't know, that is disrespectful. Children must learn how to wait. They should not interrupt important adult conversations unless there is an emergency. This builds discipline, humility and character in the child. If you see a child in need of attention, you can easily pick them up and cuddle with them (silently) while still giving your man complete respect and attention.

I remember watching my friend's husband come home from work one day. He and his wife went into the other room to greet each other and have a private chat about his day. The man was obviously frustrated from some racism he had experienced at work earlier. He was telling his wife what happened and she was rubbing his back to soothe him. As I decided to leave my friend to tend to her husband, their 8 year old came in from school. My friend told her poor husband to hold on for a second, then turned to her child and allowed him to tell her all about his field trip earlier that day. This took quite a few minutes. The look on her husband's face was one that I will never forget. He picked up his keys and went for a drive to blow off steam since his wife was preoccupied. After working all day long to support his family, his wife showed him he was not the priority. How ungrateful.

This has become a touchy subject for Black women because we are used to disposable relationships. We cater to our children above all others because deep down we feel our relationship is going to come to an end anyway. Our children seem to be the best long term investment. This kind of rationale has to change. Our relationships are meant to be for a lifetime. If we work on them there is no reason why they won't last "until death do us part".

When you put your relationship first it is far more likely that the "spark" will remain. When your children move out and start their own lives you can rejoice in their independence and look forward to spending your golden years with your man. In no way does making your relationship the priority hurt the children as long as they are getting sufficient care. It actually provides them with a model for a healthy relationship when they reach adulthood.

Teach Them to Respect the Father

The best way to get a child to respect the father is by showing respect yourself. They follow your example. Watch your words, your tone and your facial expressions. The little ones are watching.

Think up ways to teach the child to value their father. You can gather your family together and show them the father's paycheck. Let them know that he worked hard for this money and that his sacrifice will allow them to get (fill in the blank with whatever they need). If they have wanted new shoes or a toy, they will be more grateful to their father for providing it.

Let them hear you admiring their father often. As the mother, you mold their thinking. If you are always commenting on how big, brave, hardworking or talented their father is, they will believe it. Anything positive that you say about their dad will increase their self-esteem. Make this a habit!

Chapter Eight: Healing the Family

I choose not to rely on doctors for anything beyond simple diagnostic tests or emergency trauma treatments such as a bullet wound or a broken bone. I know this ideology is not for everyone. Most people are more comfortable putting their faith in strangers to look after the health of their families instead of administering personalized treatment themselves. What these people don't realize is that one of the leading causes of death is classified as iatrogenic, better known as deaths caused by health practitioners or standard medical treatments. Doctors are not always the best bet for my loved ones.

This is an extreme concern to Black people in particular. We, more than any other group of people, are targeted by racist doctors and nurses as well as by money hungry pharmaceutical companies. From the horrific birth of gynecology, to the racist Tuskegee experiments, to current questionable medical trials in Africa, we should have learned not to trust these malicious quacks with our lives. Unfortunately, we are a very trusting people who are being led to slaughter due to this terminal character flaw.

We must remember that it was allopathic (Western) health practitioners who used to urge their victims to have their blood drained (a treatment called bleeding) to cure illness. Instead, this frequently led to death. Today these sadists are still using harsh, ridiculous practices like using highly toxic medications and vaccines as treatments. The effectiveness of vaccinations are questionable at best, yet we are pressured to be injected with these poison cocktails which may contain ingredients such as viruses, formaldehyde, aborted human fetus cells, animal by-products (including swine), MSG, mercury, aluminum, and ethylene glycol (antifreeze). Medications are continually recalled due to severe side effects that debilitate the unsuspecting people who blindly trusted their doctor's prescription. Many of those who are harmed are Black. Never think that Eugenics (black murder) is a thing of the past. It is alive and well, thriving in doctor's offices, hospitals and clinics throughout the country. Beware!

Every self-respecting Black woman should know basic first aid and natural non-toxic medical solutions. Unfortunately, that is not the reality today. Possessing this type of knowledge, no matter how basic, is rare and sets you apart from the crowd. This type of knowledge makes you invaluable to your man. He should know that when he has a problem you will know what to do. He should also realize that after he consults his doctor, he should come right home and consult you, because it is you who wants the best for him. Being a wise nurse is just another part of keeping your good Black man exactly where he should be - by your side.

So what can you do to begin taking back control of your family's health? I'm going to describe a few of the remedies I have personally used, as well as some that are widely known to be effective in assisting with several different issues. However, don't stop here! I am a homemaker, not a medical professional. I can only share what has worked for my friends and family. Do not take this as official medical advice. Continue to study and try different therapies until you find the right one for you. There is plenty of information available free online, and most major cities have trained herbalists who are more than happy to consult with you. Some natural methods work immediately. On the other hand, there are some which take time to build up in the body and should be used in conjunction with dietary improvement.

The first thing you must understand is the body heals itself. Think about the last time you got a paper-cut. Didn't the skin regenerate itself? All you had to do was keep it clean. It's exactly the same with all major degenerative diseases, as well as most of the minor ailments we deal with daily. It is easy to turn to natural remedies for a "quick cure" but in order to enjoy maximum effectiveness you must start by changing your diet (see chapter 5). This lays a basic foundation for a body that is not excessively toxic. Toxicity due to bad living (processed food, drugs, alcohol, lack of exercise, promiscuity, and negative attitude) is the main reason for your aches and pains. This can be reversed by changing the way you live.

Colds, Respiratory Issues, Detoxification & Stronger Erections

Spicy Lemonade: This drink is pretty much a "cure all". The ingredients sound as though they wouldn't have a pleasant taste, but it actually isn't bad at all. Get in the habit of drinking a glass of spicy lemonade every day when you wake up in the morning. It will flush out the toxins that accumulated in your body overnight.

This is great for colds, flu and respiratory symptoms because the lemon and cayenne break up excess mucous. Mucous accumulation is what makes you miserable during colds. This also makes it a great drink for detoxification and/or fasting. I have fasted using this lemonade for up to 10 days with no problems (besides constantly daydreaming about ice cream). Anytime I feel the least bit "not right" I immediately begin continually drinking my lemonade and I'm back to my normal self in no time. You should also eliminate meat and dairy products at the first sign of a cold because they produce mucous.

Often erection issues are a sign of poor circulation and cardiovascular issues. Cayenne is great for circulation, and because the lemonade also removes thick mucus buildup you get twice the benefit. For further information see the following section entitled Erectile Dysfunction.

So how do you make this wonderful concoction? It's very simple. I originally made this by using the recipe made famous by Stanley Burroughs in "The Master Cleanse" but over time I changed it to make it more palatable to me. Once you prepare it a few times you won't even need a recipe. You will just make it according to your taste like I do.

- The juice of 1 fresh squeezed small lemon or medium lime (no bottled lemon juice)
- 3-5 Tablespoons real maple syrup or raw honey (no artificial pancake syrup)
- 10-20 drops cayenne pepper extract (you can substitute a dash of cayenne powder)
- 8-12 oz. room temperature distilled water (you can use warm water during the winter)

Combine the lemon juice, maple syrup/honey, and cayenne in a cup. Fill the cup with water and stir until combined.

Headaches

Headaches can be tricky to alleviate because they can be caused by several things. Tension headaches may be relieved by combining and diluting a couple drops of peppermint, lime and lavender essential oils into a lotion or a neutral "carrier" oil such as coconut oil, almond oil, sunflower oil or grapeseed oil. You can then massage this mixture into the temples and on the forehead. You must be extremely careful not to get this mixture too close to the eyes. The vapors from peppermint oil are strong and if you use too much, or get too close, it may cause eye irritation. Be sure it is diluted and mixed well into your lotion or cream before using it on skin.

If the headache comes from muscle tension, such as the ones that start in the neck and move up, you can try Arnica. It comes in a cream as well as tiny tablets that dissolve under the tongue. You can use either or both. Arnica is great for pain. You should always carry it with you.

Muscle Aches

Again, Arnica cream and tablets are your friend! I always try using Arnica first because it doesn't have a strong smell. Similar to headaches, mint oil often works well to relieve muscle aches. However, you will definitely smell it, so be sure you like the fragrance of mint. Always dilute essential oils into a "carrier oil" such as grapeseed oil when applying it to skin. Essential oils are very concentrated and can be irritating if you apply them undiluted.

Nausea

Ginger is great for nausea. It can work for motion sickness, morning sickness and queasy stomachs. Some people like using Ginger as a tea. Others drink Ginger Beer. You can dilute Ginger essential oil into a "carrier oil" such as apricot oil, and apply it to your stomach. Ginger tastes great in foods. Try using it on a regular basis.

Menstrual Relief

Menstruation brings on many discomforts. Because of the discharge of blood and tissue, many women experience mild anemia and/or fatigue due to loss of nutrients. You should begin treating these symptoms by replenishing vitamins and minerals. This can be done through a quality food based vitamin (especially one containing Iron), or by consuming nutrient dense foods such as salads, fresh fruit smoothies, green drink or carrot juice. Be sure to stay hydrated as well.

Red Raspberry Tea is great for women. It helps to regulate irregular periods, decreases cramping and tones the uterus. Red Raspberry is available in capsules, extracts and teas. The tea has a mild, pleasant taste.

Clary Sage is also known to be a very effective oil to treat menstrual cramps. It balances hormones and soothes the body. Use it in bathwater or in massage oil blends. A good blend is 2 drops of Clary Sage and 2 drops of Lavender Essential oil diluted in about a teaspoon of "carrier oil" such as almond oil. Rub it near the uterus as needed.

Toothache

Most toothaches can be stopped within a few seconds by rubbing a drop of Clove oil on the painful area. Clove oil has a very strong taste, so don't use more than 1 drop or you will be hurrying to try to wash the taste out of your mouth. This works just as well, if not better than commercial toothache products.

Acne/Blemishes

Red Clover Tea is an excellent blood purifier. The skin is a clear indication of the state of toxicity in the body. By cleansing the blood your skin will not only become clear, but it will begin to have a radiant glow. Red Clover is available in extracts, capsules and teas. The tea has a mild, pleasant flavor so don't be afraid to try it. After taking Red Clover 2-3 times a day consistently for 4-6 weeks (or less) you will begin to see a drastic difference in your appearance. Be sure you are maintaining basic hygiene standards as well.

Another great way to detoxify and clear the skin is by fasting. You can do a short water fast, a juice fast or use the "spicy lemonade" recipe mentioned earlier in this chapter. Fasting will cure many ailments.

One last suggestion is to also take a constipation remedy (see below) twice a week for a few weeks. If your skin is breaking out, there is a good chance that you are constipated.

Constipation

Frequent constipation indicates that your diet needs work. Eating highly refined foods (especially white flour products) as well as consumption of meat creates constipation. You can begin to reduce this by introducing more high fiber foods such as whole grains, fruits, veggies and navy beans into your diet. This will help add bulk to your stools, making elimination easier. The navy bean soup recipe in chapter 5 works well.

If you suffer from occasional constipation you can try herbal remedies such as Smooth Move tea, Senna or Cascara Segrada. These are fine to use from time to time, however, you don't want to start using them frequently. Overuse can weaken the bowel muscles. Take these herbal remedies when you have a lot of spare time. Often, they can take many hours to kick in, but when they do, you definitely want to be home.

Prune juice is known to end constipation. You can make it taste better by blending it in a smoothie with frozen bananas (also a laxative), honey and vanilla bean. Fruit smoothies in general (strawberry, mango, peach, pineapple, etc.) will help keep you regular and energized.

Physical activity promotes normal bowel function. Be sure to get some type of exercise daily. You can start walking more, taking steps instead of elevators, or do a short stretch and warm up routine in the morning (pushups, sit ups, jumping jacks, arm circles, squats, etc.).

Lastly, American toilets are designed horribly. The most natural position during a bowel movement is to squat. This allows gravity to do its thing. To recreate this in your bathroom, buy a small plastic step stool. Place this directly in front of the toilet and put your feet on it to imitate squatting. Pull your knees towards your chest if needed. This should assist in proper elimination of feces.

Cleansing your colon with colonics works well in conjunction with fasting, cleansing and cleaning up your diet. It speeds up the purification process when you help your body rid itself of old putrefied feces. However, it should not be done habitually.

Men's Wellness

This section is very important since this book is about keeping your man. If you want to "keep your man" you have to keep your man healthy! Even if he doesn't want to leave you, death is final and we have little power to stop it once it comes calling. Prevention is everything. Some of the major things men suffer from are prostate issues, sexual issues and heart issues.

Saw Palmetto is a widely recognized herb used in the treatment and prevention of prostate disorders. It nourishes the prostate and helps it remain healthy. It should be used before things get bad, but if things have already started to deteriorate it's not too late. This herb is fairly inexpensive and widely available. I recently heard of a new product being marketed on Black radio that contains Saw Palmetto. I'm skeptical because the health of Black men has never been genuinely pushed in our community. My recommendation is to stick to pure Saw Palmetto.

Another good herb to start with is Hawthorne. This nourishes and strengthens the heart muscle. The heart is one of the few organs that never get a rest. We depend on it to beat every minute of every day. Being a Black man in a society dominated by a white supremacy system adds stress to the heart. Feeding the heart is one of the best things you can do for your man besides letting him live in peace.

Zinc is a good supplement for men to take. It is essential for male hormonal health. Zinc is a nutrient which is lost during ejaculation. This can lead to premature aging. When shopping for vitamins, don't automatically look for the cheapest brand. Generally, you get what you pay for. Not all vitamins are able to be absorbed by the body so choose quality. Be sure that the brand you choose is made from an organic food base. This is easier for the body to assimilate and use.

Erectile Dysfunction

Years ago I worked for an herbal medicine company that specialized in erectile dysfunction (ED). The products were great, but the company was extremely corrupt. I checked the records as part of my job. I came across many people I knew in real life who used the product! I was shocked at the amount of people dealing with this issue. Working there showed me just how much of a problem erectile dysfunction is. Predictably, the majority of callers were middle aged white men. However, there were a surprising number of Black men calling in, especially our 20-30 year old brothers who should still be in their prime. It was then that I started trying to figure out ways to help men with this condition.

Unfortunately, because Black men live such unhealthy, unbalanced lives, many young and middle aged men have problems achieving and maintaining erections. The fact that women have stopped cooking for their families plays a major role in this epidemic. This is really sad, for them and us. Many times this impotence is an early warning sign of circulation problems or of Diabetes. If this occurs frequently, make sure he gets checked out.

Cayenne is an excellent herb for all cardiovascular/circulation issues, including ED. If there is a blood flow issue in the penis, there is blood flow issues throughout the body. Add cayenne pepper to his food as a seasoning. In addition, give it to him in vegetarian capsules (available at health food stores) or make him a Spicy lemonade drink (recipe listed earlier in chapter 8) every morning.

If the problem is Diabetes then he must strictly adhere to a healthy whole foods vegetarian diet. Cinnamon works as a blood sugar stabilizer, but you will still need to monitor this condition closely. Add cinnamon to food (this is common in ethnic menus such as Indian food) or serve him unsweetened cinnamon tea. Be sure to stay away from breads and starchy foods if you have Diabetes. Starch turns to sugar in the body. That means that a slice of bread will have a similar impact as a small portion of cheesecake.

If your man suffers from ED, he should switch to a vegetarian, vegan or raw foods diet at least until his condition improves. It is better to continue the new diet as long as possible though. Try serving him navy bean soup (recipe in chapter 5) as a replacement to his meal once or twice a day until you see improvement. It generally doesn't take long. If your man is desperate to find a solution he probably won't give you too much argument. Navy beans are a great treatment for sexual issues and many other disorders. They are extremely high in fiber and vital nutrients.

Carrot juice is also excellent for erectile dysfunction. Though it is very sweet, carrot juice tends to act as a blood sugar stabilizer. It also helps blood pressure by maintaining a healthy cholesterol level. Carrot juice boosts your energy, which is definitely a plus during sexual activity. Fresh carrot juice tastes good. Try to avoid bottled carrot juice. Pasteurization kills some of the healing properties and makes it taste strange. Begin drinking this daily. You will probably be hooked.

These suggestions really do help. I used to give this advice to people all the time. My husband overheard me, and then started telling this to his young friends who had this issue. He likes to "steal my thunder" (smile). Everyone who followed these tips improved very quickly. Once you get this issue under control it is your duty to be intelligent about what you cook for him. Study, research and find recipes that won't harm him.

High Blood Pressure/Cardiovascular

There are many natural elixirs that can help with High Blood Pressure (HBP). You can use as many as you need. These foods, spices and herbs along with wise dietary choices will have you feeling great in no time.

One of my favorites is Hibiscus tea. Not only does it taste great, but it has a pretty red color and works well in helping lower blood pressure.

Cayenne can also assist the regulation of blood flow and prevention of blood clots. It can even help treat heart attack or stroke until the ambulance arrives. At the first sign of heart attack or stroke add a teaspoon of Cayenne powder to a cup of warm or room temperature water and drink as much as possible. Repeat if necessary. You can also apply Cayenne extract under the tongue. Use as many drops as you can stand, every few minutes until you can get help. After a heart attack or stroke, use this herb frequently to season your food. You should add it towards the end of cooking for maximum effect. You don't want the heat of cooking to lessen the healing qualities of this powerful herb at all. Using this herb may help prevent the next heart attack or stroke.

Garlic and Onion are known to reduce blood pressure. They make food taste great so cook with them as much as possible. You will be adding flavor and good health! Some people don't like the texture of onions. If that is the case, you should try shredding or grating them finely instead of slicing or chopping.

Hawthorne (mentioned above) also treats blood pressure.

Cardamom is a spice used commonly in Indian cuisine which is great for HBP.

Cinnamon is good for both HBP and Diabetes. Use it in cooking or drink it as a tea.

Essential Oils such as Lavender are very calming. Creating a tranquil mood is great for the heart. Pure Lavender oil is unisex. It is only when you buy fake Lavender perfume oils or beauty products that you get a corrupt lavender scent that smells ultra-feminine. Always make sure you are purchasing 100% pure essential oils.

Smoking

Lobelia is an herb commonly used to help people quit smoking. It helps soothe the urge to smoke and often even makes the taste of cigarettes repulsive. It is calming and relaxing. This is a good aide for people who are serious about quitting. It is best to take this herb with food.

Vision

Carrot juice works great for correcting vision. The high concentration of beta carotene (provitamin A) which gives carrots their color also nourishes the eyes. Carrot juice has a surprisingly smooth, sweet taste. Even if you hate carrots, you might really enjoy fresh carrot juice. If for some strange reason you don't like it, try juicing it along with a little ginger root or an apple. Drink as much as you like. I'd start with 3 glasses a day and then slowly increase if desired. You will notice that after a few months you will need your glasses less and less. Carrot juice is also great for fasting and energy.

Sinus Infections/Allergies

Neti pots are great for cleansing the nose and sinuses. They can be found near the pharmacy of any drug store, and only cost between $10-15. It looks like a little plastic genie lamp. You fill it with a solution of pure water and salt, then lean over a sink and insert it into your nose. The water will flow from the neti pot through your nostril, into your sinuses, through the other nostril, then out of your nose. The water cleans out any mucous, irritants or dirt. This helps wash out infections and pollen that may cause hay fever symptoms. Use this as often as desired. Be sure to lean forward when using the neti pot. If you don't, the water may go up your nose then flow down your throat which is a weird sensation.

Oregano oil is antibacterial and antifungal. It can be helpful against sinusitis and allergies. Oregano oil is available in vegan capsules for convenience.

The spicy lemonade mentioned earlier in this chapter is great for sinus infections because it clears out mucous.

Asthma

Asthma is caused by excessive mucous in the respiratory system. This condition can be helped immensely by ridding the body of mucous. One helpful herb is mullein which comes in many forms including teas, capsules, and extracts. Another good tool is the spicy lemonade mentioned in this chapter. You should also use cayenne as a seasoning on food whenever possible. Dairy and meat cause mucous formation so asthmatics should strive to avoid all dairy products and lessen meat consumption. If the asthma is severe, a strict vegetarian diet is strongly recommended.

Chapter Nine: Divine Beauty

Never underestimate the power of a beautiful woman. How you present yourself to the world is extremely important. Your look gives society its first impression of you, be it good or bad. All wise women take time to ensure that they are well put together before leaving their home. Even in the home you should always be presentable, in spite of the fact that you may be alone. Look good for yourself! It builds self-esteem and self-confidence.

When it comes to beauty for Black women, less is more. We have more natural coloring in our skin than other ethnicities. This creates natural shades and highlights which are what makeup tries to mimic. The more cosmetics we use, the more we take away from our natural beauty. Other groups of women need these cosmetics just to look presentable. I miss the days when they didn't have quality make up for Black women. We looked much better back then without it. All the Black woman really needs to look good is a healthy diet, good hygiene and right living.

The first step in being attractive Black women is realizing our own beauty. We must really believe that Black is best. This is difficult because many of us have been told that our Black features are not attractive at some point in our lives. On some level we believe it. Black women must now look in the mirror and fall in love with ourselves. We must look at other Black women and recognize their beauty too (in a wholesome way). Black women must completely embrace our natural features in order to truly consider ourselves mentally healthy. Every Black woman has a beautiful feature that can be enhanced. Even a "plain Jane" may have unique eyes, full lips or a beautiful smile that lights up the room. Don't be your own worst critic. We are the epitome of beauty from our sun kissed skin to our thick, curly hair.

Most well-balanced Black men (not the ones who are brain-dead) prefer a more natural, low maintenance woman. They want you to be able to get your hair wet, be active and have fun. They don't like your face to be so colorful it resembles a clown. The fake eyelashes we wear can be horrific when not applied tastefully. Fake fingernails and toenails that look like claws are not a good choice. The weaves with Crayola colors are evidence that you are doing way too much. The goal is to enhance your beauty, not morph into a Rainbow Brite figurine. It's no wonder young people think these things are cute considering their role models are women like Nikki Minaj and Lil Kim. Always remember, Black men like women with flavor, not tackiness.

So what can you do to enhance what God gave you without going overboard? I am not a cosmetologist, but here are a few things I recommend.

Skin Care

Beautiful skin has more to do with what you put in your body than what you put on it. An abundance of water and a diet of whole foods are crucial to looking radiant. As I mentioned earlier, constipation plays a major role in blemishes and acne. When the body is unable to rid itself of toxins through defecation it will push them out by any means necessary. Unfortunately, this usually comes out through the skin. Water, exercise, whole foods and the herbs mentioned in Chapter 8 will help with this.

Luckily for us, Black skin ages very slowly when we live a righteous lifestyle. Don't waste your time and money on anti-aging products. As a matter of fact, you don't need to spend a lot of money on any skin products when you are eating right.

- You can use a mild liquid soap or organic cleanser to clean your face. Avoid heavy perfumes and a long list of chemicals.
- Sea salt can be used to exfoliate. You can also use a very gentle organic face scrub. You should exfoliate your body at least once

a week to remove grime and dead skin cells. This will give you a radiant look.
- Witch hazel makes an excellent toner to balance the skin. You should use a toner after washing your face but before moisturizing.
- You can try coconut oil, whipped shea butter, cocoa butter or mango butter to moisturize your face and body. To keep your hands and feet soft in cold weather you can apply shea butter before bed then put on a pair of thick socks and gloves (not gloves that have been worn outside). When you wake up your skin will be much softer.
- There are several natural clay masks that pull the dirt from deep in you pores. Look for one at your local health food store. Feel free to add a few drops of lavender or lemon oil to your mask for acne prevention. I have also seen masks made of dried, ground orange peels which work great. Citrus is good for acne prone skin.
- Try steaming your face once or twice a week. This will open the pores and help you sweat out any impurities. All you need to do is fill a big pot with water, cover it and let it boil. Once it boils, take the lid off and lean over it. Drape a towel over your head to trap in the stream. I usually stay under the towel for about 20 minutes or so. I like to play music while steaming my face to avoid boredom. This is great for clearing the complexion.
- Be sure to use the same routine on your neck and collarbone as you do on your face. That area is visible too!
- Exercise is great for the skin! It helps you sweat out toxins and keeps your skin shining.
- To lighten birthmarks or blemishes apply equal parts of lemon and oregano oils once or twice a day. Stop using this mixture or dilute it if irritation occurs. This will help fade dark spots over time. This mixture works for small areas. DO NOT use this to try to bleach your skin. If you are a dark complexioned woman, rejoice! You have been blessed with the most stunning shade of skin. Don't waste your time trying to downgrade yourself to showcase remnants of self-hatred.

Once your skin is shiny and bright you may choose to enhance your best features. Again, we aren't trying to morph into something we're not. We are embracing ourselves. One of the most important things in my regimen is making sure my eyebrows are well groomed. I prefer to get them threaded. This is an Indian custom, but it leaves your eyebrows impeccable. You may also choose to get them waxed, plucked or shaved with a razor. If you only have a few out of place hairs, feel free to tweeze them yourself. If you have the Al B. Sure (unibrow) look, go to a professional for best results.

The eyebrows are very important because they frame the eyes the way a picture frame displays a photo. The eyes are usually one of the most exotic, beautiful features on a woman's face. This is why I advise you to stick with very subtle eyeliner or kohl if you must wear makeup. Kohl has been used for thousands of years to line the eyes similar to western eyeliner. However, kohl is applied to the inside of the eyelid whereas eyeliner lines around the outside of the eye. To complete the look you could try a soft colored natural lip gloss. If not, at least some use some Burt's Beeswax, Carmex or Chapstick. There is nothing worse that a woman with crusty lips! Stay away from blood red and harsh fuchsia lip colors. Please (yes I'm begging) don't use a black liner on your lips. Use organic products whenever possible. Traditional cosmetics contain toxic, disgusting, Cancer-causing chemicals.

I prefer essential oils and perfume oils to perfume. Perfumes tend to evaporate. Oils last much longer. Perfumes are also rumored to contain several cancer causing ingredients that manufacturers are not required to list. You don't want your scent to be overpowering so be sure to apply your oil in minute amounts. You should smell good all over, not just on your neck. This means applying the oil in more than one place. Since we have men, we have to place the oil strategically because they can have an unpleasant taste. Try placing a few drops behind the ears, near the armpits, under each breast (not in between them), near the navel, the lower back, on the inside of the elbows, the wrists, high on the inner thighs, the back of the knees and the bottom of the feet. This will give you an even scent and avoid popular foreplay spots as much as possible. Be sure to wear a nice fragrance to bed, not just during the day. Bedtime is the most important time to smell sweet.

Avoid tattoos. Nine times out of ten you will regret them as you mature. Getting random tattoos was popularized due to jail culture and is not a good choice for refined women. Please don't be offended if you have tattoos. I made the mistake of getting one myself as a teenager. If you must get one, be sure it's in a place that can be easily hidden and get a design that has some cultural significance. Be sure it's not a person's name. It would be far better to get a henna design instead of inking up your body permanently. Tattoos put you at risk for several blood-borne diseases. If you want color in your hair, try henna for reddish highlights or indigo for a dark blue-black color. Be careful not to stain your bathroom if you do it yourself. Make sure you get authentic henna/indigo that can be safely used on the skin. Don't get cheap imitations. Henna is natural and actually helps condition the hair. It is not permanent.

The Natural Hair Controversy

I cut off my relaxed hair 7 years ago. I didn't want to keep putting chemicals in my hair and I didn't understand why I started getting relaxers in the first place. I realized it was ridiculous to change any part of my appearance to be thought of as "acceptable", "a dime" or whatever other slang terms were out at the time. I felt then, as I do now, people can either love me or leave me alone. I'm not changing. I love me. When I say I'm beautiful or I love myself, please don't confuse this with conceit. Black women, we should love ourselves. We are beautiful! We must truly recognize our own value. Sisters, begin to love you!

Many Black militants say Black women perm and color their hair just to look white. I'm not sure if I agree with that. Now, if you have a long, stringy blonde weave that looks like Brittany Spears, you have some explaining to do. Otherwise, there are many reasons we continue to get relaxers. None of them justify it. Here are a few:

- Black women like to be unique. We will try all kinds of things to stand out. We often take this way too far.
- Many of us have had relaxers since pre-school. That is all we know. We are clueless how to take care of our natural hair. We may not even know how our natural hair looks or feels. We don't put a lot of thought into it. We just do what we've always done.
- Some of us think natural hair is too hard to manage. We are not familiar with how to properly care for it.
- Some of us really do want to look as non-Black as possible. We might not be aiming for white, but we wouldn't be upset if we passed for Hispanic or mixed race.

The reason I hesitate to jump on the "white girl wannabe" bandwagon is because it is not true for all people. For instance, I used to color my hair a brownish/reddish color because I felt my dark hair made me look pale. I (mistakenly) thought these wild colors would make me look a shade or two darker. Looking back, it was not flattering at all. Also, during my childhood I had a jheri curl long after it was considered cute. I jumped at the opportunity to get a perm to make my hair "look decent." I would've agreed to braids if that was offered as an option. My goal wasn't looking European. I just wanted to be pretty and not be teased.

We must consider the sisters with green, pink, blue and purples weaves. Those colors are not put in to look white. I'm not sure exactly why they are put in, other than being a desperate cry for attention and help (smile). That being said, I don't feel comfortable making sweeping generalizations as far as the need to look white. However, I do feel that white supremacy is at the root of us not respecting ourselves enough to realize when we look ridiculous.

Regardless of why we do it, we must stop allowing toxic chemicals to be absorbed into our scalps in an attempt to fit into the mold that other people have created for us. Our hair texture is exclusively designed to adorn our faces. Black women look much better and more unique once they lose the chemicals. Flat hair doesn't flatter our broad features like a cute afro, braids or locs do. It is just a matter of finding the styles that best suit you. There are plenty to choose from. We need to end the cycle so our children are not exposed to the same nonsense we were. Even if you relax your hair, please don't do that to your child. Never speak of nappy hair as if it is a bad thing.

Some women are afraid they will be classified as a lesbian, militant or naturalist/vegetarian if they decide to go natural. Sometimes people do make these ignorant assumptions. The truth is you don't have to be any of these stereotypes to wear your hair the way God intended. You don't have to join a clique or ask permission to be yourself. It is your right to have your natural allure accepted and respected. It is a great feeling when you genuinely accept yourself in totality. Black hair is beautiful!

How to Dress

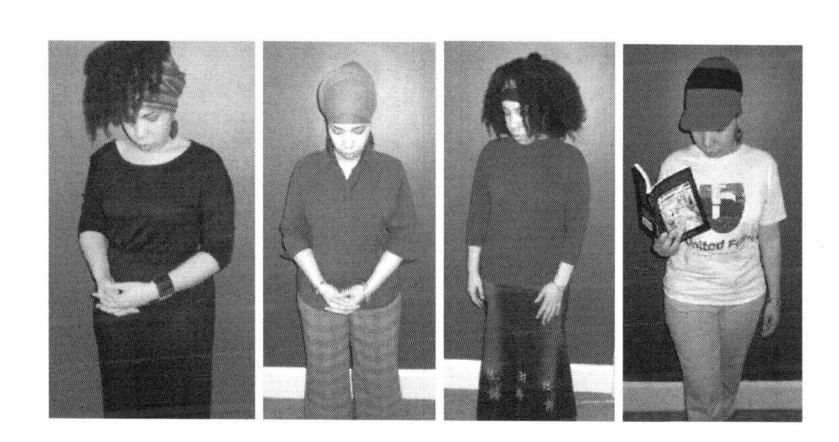

Black woman, put some clothes on! We can tell you are fine without you showing every nook and cranny. We must begin to develop modesty and shame about coming out of the house half naked. This is not a sign of liberation. This is a sign of loose morals. We can never expect respect from anyone when we don't respect ourselves enough to cover up. I know it's a "free country" but we are cheapening our beautiful Black selves by dressing in inappropriate ways.

Some folks will try to say that because a few people in our native Africa walk around minimally clothed, that this makes it okay for us to walk around half naked. No ma'am, it doesn't. We do not live in an African society; we live amongst beasts, thugs, rapists and murderers. We do not live among Black men who will risk their lives to protect us; we live among Black men who won't even pull their pants up to protect their own rectums from abuse. A little common sense goes a long way – we aren't talking about the same environment. In most modern-day African cities, Black women are fully clothed in some of the most beautiful garments you could ever imagine.

One of the most necessary steps that women should take when looking for a good Black man is to dress modestly. Only indecent men are attracted to indecent women. That's one reason so many Black women claim they attract "dogs". If you are using fresh meat as bait every stray dog in the neighborhood is going to sniff around.

Once we get a man we should remain covered in public. Your body should be for his eyes only. No one else has earned the privilege to see your goodies. Men innately love to look at women's bodies. Why give complete strangers a free peep show? Don't cheapen yourself Black woman. If you go to any jewelry store you will see that all of the diamonds are kept behind a glass. They may keep faux jewelry out on display though. Why?

> **Helpful Hint:** *Diamonds are stored away because jewelers don't want masses of people having access to their most valuable pieces. This is true of all prized possessions. You are*

worth more than a shiny rock. Act like it! Covering your body shows respect for your man and it protects him as well.

There was a woman who had an unusually voluptuous figure and she loved to show it off. Her man would often ask her to tone down her outfits. She would always start a huge fight and accuse him of being jealous. They were going out one day and she decided to wear a low cut blouse and pants so tight, I know she had to jump to get in them (y'all know what I'm talking about). Her man was tired and didn't feel like arguing that night so he decided to remain silent. They went to a local restaurant to get some food. Some dudes standing outside stared at her breasts as she walked in. Her man glared at them to get them to back down. After they picked up the food, the men stared at her behind as she walked out. The man was angry, but kept quiet. He figured it was her fault for dressing like that in the first place. As they walked to the car one of the men got bold and said, "Damn shawty, you got a fat booty!" At this point the brother's manhood had been stepped on enough. He couldn't let that slide even if she was dressed like a prostitute. That comment was disrespectful to her and him as well, since he was her man. He stepped to the dude and asked him why he was being disrespectful. They argued and things escalated. The disrespectful man pulled out a gun. Luckily the bullet missed. Was it worth it?

What needs to be covered? It depends on your body type. A very skinny woman may not have as much to cover as a curvy woman. At the very least, your thighs, knees, buttocks, breasts, back and stomach should be covered. I prefer ankle length skirts for myself. Keep in mind that just because your clothes are long doesn't necessarily mean they are modest. Garments shouldn't be skin tight. On the other hand, clothing shouldn't be too baggy or look sloppy. They should fit well. Tight clothes look especially bad on larger frames because they will make you look even bigger and expose any rolls or cellulite bumps. Always purchase clothes in the correct size in order to look dignified. By all means if you need a body shaper to smooth out your figure in certain fabrics, wear one!

Your apparel should have a soft, feminine look. I'm not saying you must wear pink, lace and beads, although I do. I'm just saying that you shouldn't resemble a man. There is nothing wrong with dresses and skirts. It is not against the law to wear pretty bright colors sometimes. Try to avoid heavy fabrics that men wear such as flannel or thick denim. If you do wear it, be sure that it is made in a feminine cut and color. I know people are trying to embrace androgynism these days, but it is much more attractive to look feminine, unapologetically. Try accessories like earrings, bangle bracelets, head bands, scarves and headwraps to complete the look.

Many women make the choice to cover their hair with hats, headwraps, scarves, hijabs and headpieces. This is a sign of modesty. The hair of a woman is her crown. Black hair is very attractive when styled nicely, which is why some women cover it. This decision is no different than choosing to wear a long skirt or a high neckline. When your hair is covered you tend to be respected more by men. They will greet you with a "Peace sister" instead of "Hey baby". Some religions require women to cover their hair, but some women do it for their own personal reasons. There are many ways to cover the hair in fashionable, attractive ways. Feel free to experiment with this if you want. It can be fun to mix colors and prints.

Body Weight

Black women are blessed with the best body potential. I say potential because we are ruining our bodies with laziness, gluttony and poisons. There is no woman on the planet that has better muscle tone than we do. The tragedy is that we often hide our beautiful bodies under layers of cellulite and rolls of fat. Some of us are foolish enough to think extra fat gives you better curves. The truth is, for the average Black woman, slimming down gives you far more curves than putting on the pounds. A flat stomach makes breasts look much bigger. A slim waist makes the buttocks and hips look shapelier.

We became very misguided in the early 90's when "thick" became the trend. Back in those days everyone was thin. To be "thick" was to be curvy, not obese. A good example of thick would be Salt-N-Pepa. If you look at the women on the Sir Mix-A-Lot video "Baby Got Back", not one of them was overweight. We took the appreciation that our men have for our physiques and went way too far. I am not saying you can't be attractive and still be bigger than the norm. I am saying that being unhealthy and/or sloppy is unattractive. There are women with a heavier frame who are absolutely stunning. The women who pull this off are just naturally robust, but they still work out and are in fairly good shape.

If you know you could stand to lose a few pounds, don't hesitate. Get started! I'm not suggesting you exercise solely to please your man. It's bigger than that. Besides, some of our brothers claim to like "big women" now. You should do it for yourself. It feels good to be able to move quickly, gracefully and effortlessly. It is good to put on clothes and have them fit smoothly with no lumps or bumps. It gives you confidence to know that when you get undressed in front of your man there will be no surprises in store for him. We all know how much a good pair of body shapers can hide (smile). More than anything, it puts the mind at ease to lower your risk of the long list of degenerative diseases that go along with being overweight.

The tips in this book will go a long way in helping you reach a healthy weight. There is no miracle pill. Weight loss requires you to change your habits and lifestyle. Start by taking a walk after dinner. It would be even better if you could take a walk in the morning as well. Walking is the easiest form of exercise. If you walk regularly, it will tone your whole body, not just your legs. Never feel that you need to run to get in optimal shape. Running can put unwanted stress on the joints. If all you can do is walk, that's absolutely fine! Along with increasing exercise, you must stop eating processed foods. I gave plenty of information on this in Chapter 5. If you begin changing these two areas you will see results. It might take a while, but anything worth having will take time and effort. Please don't go to extremes and develop a hard, chiseled body. Women should be soft, even when we are toned.

Basic Hygiene

You can tell a lot about a woman by the way she takes care of her body. Being dirty is a sign of low self-esteem, past abuse and/or undiagnosed mental issues. It is not natural to enjoy feeling grimy, smelly or anything less than fresh. This may seem like an unnecessary topic, but many women do not have good personal hygiene.

Most of us have had the experience of going into a bathroom stall behind someone who looks well put together, however, the stench they leave behind is HORRIFIC! You may even wonder how they keep a man with that much funk going on. The truth is, regardless of how strong the stench, they probably can't smell themselves. If you have never had an experience like this, you are in the minority. It is a fact that our nose becomes accustomed to our own scent; so many people honestly don't know they have a problem. Never think you can skip baths and no one will notice. **We do.** And perfume, oils and sprays don't hide it.

So what helps? Soap and warm water does. When you bathe you should use a natural soap. It's not that expensive. You can try a good multipurpose soap like Dr. Bronner's. Try to stay away from harsh artificial perfumes and chemicals in your soap, especially if you intend to use that soap in your genital region. Speaking of that area, commercial douches are not necessary. A warm bath 1-2 times a day works wonders. The vagina will naturally clean itself if you give it a chance. Wash yourself every time you use the restroom. Travel with wet wipes for times when you use the restroom away from home. If you have hair in that region it should be well groomed. A natural conditioner can be used to soften pubic hair, just keep it away from the internal genital area. Talcum powder has been linked to Cancer; if you must use a powder try baking soda. Wear cotton panties on a regular basis to allow the vagina to breath. Notice I didn't say "granny panties" or "period panties". There are super cute, nicely cut cotton panties on the market. Save the fancy fabrics for special occasions when you won't be wearing them long.

If you are experiencing genital odor issues there are two things to do. First, go to the doctor to make sure you don't have any disease or infection. If you are all clear there, then it's time to change your diet. Drastically reduce your meat and dairy intake. Overindulgence in meat and dairy products not only constipates you, it also causes bad body odors. If you cut those foods down and add fresh fruit juices, water and salads to your menu it will really help you have a lighter, sweeter smell. Fasting can assist as well.

Two areas that are often missed when bathing are the belly button and behind the ears. Make sure to wash them diligently because they can hold odors. Also scrub the neck well. Often sweat, grime and hair products accumulate there.

It is a myth that Black hair shouldn't be washed often. Chances are, if you are washing your hair once every 2 weeks or less, your hair probably stinks. This is especially true if you exercise or sweat, if you use grease or heavy products, and definitely if you smoke. Hair odor is something that can be very hard to detect on yourself. You should be washing your hair a minimum of once a week, and if you have natural hair, you can wash it as much as you want. Many naturals wash daily and often will just wash with conditioner (aka no-poo/ co-wash) to avoid stripping and drying out the hair. Of course, if you have very long, thick hair, washing daily may be unrealistic. However, weekly washing is not!

I suggest getting a pumice stone to use on your feet while in the tub. There is no reason to walk around in sandals with crusty, ashy feet. If you do, you are dead wrong. Even in winter, your feet should be soft, pretty and feminine. Imagine your man trying to give you a foot massage with your feet scratching up his hands and giving him calloused. Ridiculous! There should be no polish peeling off. No hammertime. No odors. Again, your feet should never stink if you are washing 1-2 times daily and your diet is reasonably pure. If somehow you still have stinky feet issues, sprinkle baking powder in your shoes. Be sure to keep your fingernails and toenails neatly trimmed and clean! Nail polish is full of toxic chemicals. A good alternative are henna dyes which are currently being marketed as colorful nail polishes. They are available online in reds, pinks, oranges and other colors. They slowly fade away instead of chipping like commercial polishes.

Breath makes a big impression. You should carry a toothbrush with you to use after every meal. Bringing floss doesn't hurt either. If you have a problem with halitosis, as always, you should examine your diet. If you still need help, you can sprinkle a drop or two of peppermint or clove essential oil on your toothbrush before brushing with your toothpaste. These oils are strong and take some getting used to. However, they leave your mouth feeling cleaner and your breath fresher. Choose non-fluoride natural toothpastes. Fluoride is a poison being used to make Americans more passive. Fluoride toothpastes often have a warning label telling you not to swallow the toothpaste. That is due to its toxicity. Realistically, you always swallow a little toothpaste residue when you brush. Don't take the chance. Don't forget to brush your tongue. I am not a fan of gum. It tastes good, but chewing it tends to make you look like a cow chewing cud. Not a good look. Carry small organic mints. If you are fasting, try whole clove buds. Clove buds help freshen the breath and moisten the mouth.

It is not just a saying that "your body is a temple". It is a fact. Do not neglect your body because of lack of time or laziness. Cleanliness is essential to health. Feeling fresh elevates your mood. It makes you more ladylike. Carrying yourself well makes you desirable. Don't be that woman who is the last to know she carries on odor. Many times no one has the heart to tell someone they lack hygiene.

I have heard lowlife men laughing about a woman they were intimate with who had a strong odor. They didn't care enough about her to let her know so she could fix it. They didn't care enough about themselves to not sleep with an unclean woman. Instead, they made her the laughing stock amongst their friends, and the poor woman never even knew. You have to love yourself. Sometimes there are major issues going on when someone lacks hygiene. Other times it comes from being raised by a mother who lacked hygiene. Either way, let's stop this trend and become truly refined. We are the best.

> ***Helpful Hint:** The easiest and most effective thing you can do to improve your appearance is to smile! Many Black women have extremely mean, uninviting expressions on their faces the majority of the time. Make an effort to look friendly and happy. Use your pretty smile to brighten up your family's day!*

It is not a cliché when I say being beautiful inside is just as important as being beautiful outside. There are many "classically pretty" women whose personalities make them repulsive. There are an equal amount of women who may look a bit plainer, but are absolutely irresistible to men. They are what Maya Angelou writes about in her famous poem "Phenomenal Woman". A Black woman who is full of energy, joy and love, having a big smile and a sparkle in her eyes can make you overlook any perceived flaws. She is fun to be around. She always has something nice to say. She makes you feel good. This beautiful demeanor is something we all need to improve on no matter how pretty we think we are. It is not something that can be faked. It comes from being genuinely satisfied and content with your life.

Chapter Ten: Do Good Men Cheat?

Answer: Sometimes.

There are many things to consider when faced with this issue. It takes two to make a marriage work. We must first be honest and look to see what part, if any, we played in the betrayal. I know it's not the typical "angry Black woman/go slash his tires" type answer you may want to hear. I don't advocate craziness (complete immaturity) but I do condone honesty.

An instance of infidelity does not automatically mean the end of a relationship. I know that we claim it does, but in reality, most women choose to stay in the relationship. We might as well look at this situation realistically. We are living in a modern Babylon. Women of all races are walking around practically naked. We have sex as if we are shaking hands. Women have become very aggressive in initiating acts of fornication and adultery. Even married women won't take no for an answer. America is a cesspool of low morals, diseases and dysfunction. It's not unreasonable to see how a good man could get "caught up" if he's not careful. Does this excuse the behavior? Of course not!

I grew up almost exclusively around men. All of them were cheaters at some point. Some cheated habitually. Others cheated because they were young, but stopped as they got older. Some cheated until they found a girl they really liked. Some were faithful until they no longer got along with their partner. Others were usually faithful except for the so-called occasional "accidental" one night stand. As you can see, there was a lot of cheating going on!

As the only female in my immediate family besides my mother, I was able to observe many male personalities from the fairly "good man" to the straight up "man-whore". I will say that as they matured they all became much more likely to be faithful. When assessing whether or not your relationship is worth saving consider this:

- Was your man being physically satisfied at home?
- Were you constantly angry, disrespectful, argumentative or condescending towards him?
- Did he get enough attention from you?
- Did you make him your top priority?
- Did you create a good home environment?
- Did you ADMIRE him and make him feel like a man?
- Did you cook on a regular basis or did he come home to peanut butter sandwiches?
- Was it a one-time thing or ongoing? How long? How many women?
- Were they tested for STD's? Did they use condoms?
- What was the level of violation? Was she in your house? Was she around your children?
- Who did he cheat with? Did you know her? Are you related?
- Was she Black?

The list of things to consider goes on and on. Be honest, have you been the best mate you could be? Did you let gripes with him knock you off your pedestal? Is he a serial philanderer with no intentions of changing?

Watching the men I was surrounded by convinced me that males, especially alpha males, are naturally polygamous. That doesn't mean that "cheating" is okay or destined to occur. It just means that it may be a struggle for them at times. Knowing this means you must do your part. Every person is responsible for their own actions; however, as his partner you have a duty to do what you can to help him stay on the right path.

So what kinds of things can you do? The same things I've been talking about for the last 9 chapters! Weren't you paying attention? Just kidding.

Here are some things to keep in mind:

- Men need sex like women need water. It is a basic physical need for them. Some say women like sex as much as men. That's true! But we generally don't need it as much as they do, no matter how much we may want it. You should try not to reject your man's sexual advances unless there is good reason. What if you are not in the mood? That's understandable. However, at least give him a chance to try to get you in the mood. He will probably succeed, and he more than likely won't require some long episode anyway. He'll usually be happy with whatever you give him; so make it long or make it short, but don't turn him away. You might start off saying it will be quick but change your mind in the heat of passion. Who knows? Either way, don't neglect this vital part of your relationship.
- As I've said over and over, men have a need to feel admired. Love is a basic need for women to function well in a relationship. Just as you desire love, he desires admiration and respect! Always notice him and compliment him. Contrary to popular belief, many good men are not lured away because the sex with the new woman is better. As a matter of fact, you've had time to learn his body and its responses, so the sex probably isn't better (physically)! The easiest way to manipulate a man into "cheating" is by flattery and ego stroking. It makes him feel manly and attractive. It's exciting to be wanted and exalted, that's what makes it good. We leave him vulnerable to this when we stop admiring him. Don't let this happen to you.
- A man wants peace. He does not want to be around a loud, nagging, argumentative, psycho. He wants a pleasant, sweet, soft spoken woman to whisper sweet words in his ear and take care of his needs. If you are busy trying to burn him with hot, greasy skillets and run over his momma with your truck just to prove how angry (immature) you are, he will either leave or cheat.... or cheat for a while and then leave. Grow up and start presenting yourself in an intelligent manner.
- Have you kept up your appearance? Do you walk around in raggedy non-matching pajamas full of holes? Have you gained 80 lbs. in 4 years? Do you wear headwraps only to avoid running

a comb through your hair? Men are visual. They want to see a pretty woman who takes care of herself. It is hard for a man to take pride in you if you look unkempt! Don't fool yourself; you are no one's fantasy looking like that no matter how pretty your face might be.

- Are you too inhibited to let him see your body? As I just said above, men are visual. They love to look at women's bodies. Once he makes a commitment to be faithful to you, he feels he has a right to see your figure. He's absolutely right! If he can't look at you, who is he supposed to look at? The one he starts cheating with! If you are not happy with your body then start eating right and exercising. Following the dietary advice in this book and going on a daily walk should help out a lot. Get yourself together, but in the meantime, give that poor brother something to look at! Believe me, as a woman you are usually your own worst critic. He doesn't see many of the "flaws" that bother you. Even if your religion requires modesty, that does not extend to your private space. When you come home, take off that long dress and show him your "Secrets". I said "Secrets" not "Fruit of the Looms", in case I wasn't clear enough the first time.

So when is it safe to call it a wrap, pack his stuff (or your stuff) and be done with it? Only you know that answer. Some things that may tip the scale include:

- Can you forgive? Some women really can't get over the betrayal of infidelity. If you want to have a successful relationship, you must be able to move on. This means not bringing it up constantly, not retaliating, not holding a grudge and not being overly suspicious of him. This is not an easy thing to do! If you feel like you will not be able to get over his indiscretions in a reasonable amount of time, you should probably leave now.
- Is he basically a good man or is he a pimp or playboy? If you have a good man who handles his responsibilities, is a good father and a good provider but he just slipped up, it may be worth saving the relationship. If deep down you know he is using you, he doesn't really care for you, the love is gone or he won't stop playing the field, it might be time to end things.

- Is he honest? Some men in our community have decided to become openly polygamous. I respect them much more than I respect a liar. At least they are honest and give you a choice of agreeing or leaving. The problem is Black people in general have become very irresponsible and immature. Polygamy sounds great in theory, but it seldom works when carried into practice among Black people in America. The majority of the men promoting this are just playing games and trying to justify and legitimize "big pimpin'". You know better than me if he is sincere and capable of managing several relationships, and if you want to be a part of that and the drama that comes with it.
- Is he trying to convince you to engage in "3 ways" or "ménage et trois" encounters? Not only is he still looking for ways to be unfaithful, but he's being outright disrespectful. My vote would be to tell him you don't swing that way, and drop him as quickly as possible. His mind is not right.
- Is he remorseful? I don't mean fake tears and an Oscar-worthy performance. After you find out, you talk and everything calms down, does he feel bad? Even if you played a role in him having an affair, does he regret his actions? Is he disappointed in himself? Would he make a better decision next time? Has this experience opened up the lines of communication? Believe it or not, some men feel no remorse and don't even pretend to feel remorse for the pain they've caused you. No remorse is definitely a bad sign.

In closing, some people can fully recover from this situation. Others are scarred forever. Neither reaction is wrong. The best advice I can give is to prevent it from happening in the first place. Don't morph from the person he met into a stranger. Don't get too comfortable. Don't let yourself go. Don't stop talking. Don't stop touching. Don't hold each other hostage in marriage. This doesn't guarantee you will never have to confront this issue, but it makes it far less likely.

If you choose to stay, focus your time on improving yourself and your relationship. It isn't fair to make baseless accusations without good reason or evidence. Do not waste time spying on your man. Trust is vital in a relationship. Let him rebuild your trust in him.

I would be naïve if I addressed infidelity without speaking about the trend of unfaithful females. Today, women cheat as much as men. We are promiscuous for various reasons including revenge, bartering (sex for material goods), emotional trauma, sexual dissatisfaction within the relationship, or a lack of ethics. We must stop engaging in such lowlife behavior if we expect to be respected. There is never a good reason to use sex as revenge. Being unprincipled hurts you just as much as it hurts your partner. It is better to leave a relationship than to lose your honor. Giving sexual favors in exchange for possessions is a form of prostitution. Your body is worth more than getting bills paid or a cheap release of tension. The trend of easy sex is ruining our race. It is creating unstable homes, spreading disease and making trust impossible. A steady stream of open legs has lowered the bar for men. This is one reason that it may be difficult to find a good one.

> *Helpful Hint:* **Unless he understands and respects the gift of heaven that is between your legs, do not allow any man to enter your vagina. Good women respect their womb, spirit and integrity too much to cheat or be promiscuous.**

Chapter Eleven: If You Can't Get Along in Peace

If you still can't get along in peace after practicing the advice in this book, it may be time to separate. It is ideal to stay together. That should always be your goal. However, Black people need peace. We cannot function in chaotic environments where arguing, verbal abuse, physical abuse, hatred and disrespect are the norm. Those things cause stress which can be deadly. A dysfunctional relationship is not worth your life.

- Try not to feel overly guilty. In many cultures separation or divorce is unspeakable and shameful. It should be. Nevertheless, we have not had the benefits of any rites of passage or training on how to pick good mates and be good partners. Many of our relationships are doomed from the beginning by a lack of knowledge.
- When there is still a decent level of love and respect a union can be saved. The catch is that both people have to want to save it. When you begin to make changes your man might resist. He may think you are suddenly being nice just to manipulate him. He may be so used to speaking to you harshly that it has become habitual. Give this philosophy time to work. When you slip, get back up and start again. You will certainly make mistakes. Be patient with him and yourself.
- Many times we make a poor choice from the beginning. Unless we have guidance from wise elders, we tend to select spouses for our own immature reasons. We don't know how to test a man. We do not see how character flaws will affect the relationship down the line. Many times fundamental things are overlooked for superficial things. Sometimes these things can be hashed out. Sometimes they can't.

*In the following stories names have been changed to protect the guilty.

Failure to Perform Your Duty

I knew a couple we'll call Brandon and Kristen. Kristen noticed that Brandon talked as if he was big and bad from a distance, but was much calmer and quieter in person. She liked feeling that she brought out the "tender side" of him. Brandon gained her interest by saying he was beginning to embrace her religious philosophy, but in reality he had no proven track record. These would've been warning signs to an intelligent woman - but not to an easily impressed nineteen year old girl like Kristen. The positives were that Brandon appeared to be a nice guy for the most part. He didn't cuss or raise his voice. His single mother had raised him with decent manners. He had a good job. He was a bit of a book fanatic like Kristen, so they got along well as friends. They assumed "romantic love" would follow. It didn't.

Everything was okay for a little while. They traveled, bought a few properties and established their domestic routine. Soon some things started to bother Kristen. Kristen felt Brandon's mother was a bit overbearing and meddled too much, considering he was in his late twenties. He also had a bit of a "wandering eye" and claimed he wasn't really attracted to women of Kristen's complexion.

The worst thing was when she began to question his manhood. Kristen started to realize that this "bad boy" image was just a façade. One day they were walking by a university after going out to eat. A group of about six to seven scrawny white boys from the university walked down the same sidewalk they were on. Instead of moving to the proper side they took over the majority of the sidewalk. Brandon sped up to walk in front of Kristen to give the white boys more space to pass. Even in single file, the couple still didn't have enough room to walk by comfortably. Kristen had a completely different temperament than Brandon did. Since she saw they weren't going to move she decided not to move either. Kristen prepared for impact and made sure to drive her shoulder into the white boy as hard as possible. When he looked at her crazy she called him a "cracker" and kept walking. Brandon saw none of this because he had his back turned while walking ahead. He wouldn't have done anything even if he had seen it.

This infuriated Kristen. Her father raised her to expect protection from all Black males, not just her own. Kristen's father opened doors, walked beside her or with her in clear view, and never sat with his back to a door, so he could always see what was going on. It was unfathomable to her that this big Black male had left her unprotected. She lost a lot of respect for him that day. She also made the mistake of calling him quite a few emasculating names and a few profanities. I don't think she regretted it though.

Later on another incident happened. They went to buy a car from a guy they vaguely knew. They both wanted to keep their current vehicle, but the salesman kept trying to be slick and give them quotes using their car as a trade in. They said, "Never mind" and went home. Brandon and Kristen got a call later that week saying they were able to jumble the numbers to get them the price they wanted without a trade in. The salesman said they'd even pick the couple up to come sign the paperwork as a courtesy. Brandon said okay and they went to the dealership. Once they got there they were forced to wait an unreasonably long time. Kristen was getting slightly annoyed. Once they got to speak to the finance guy (an Indian) she realized this was the same raggedy offer as before. Kristen turned to Brandon and quietly told him the sales guy was being shady. This Indian man must've forgotten he wasn't in India. He actually yelled at her saying "No one in this office is shady!" First she looked at Brandon, stunned. He was looking down at the floor. Kristin had to stop herself from putting her hands on the reckless Indian. Needless to say, after she said what was on her mind, he backed down and apologized with his tail between his legs. Brandon bought the car anyway.

Things like this would happen from time to time, causing Kristen to lose most of her respect for Brandon. The primary duties of a man are to protect and provide. Doing 50% doesn't cut it. For all his tough talk Kristen even told him once that she felt if they were walking down the street and got robbed she would have to defend him. She was joking, but serious at the same time. This is a situation where you should leave.

Helpful Hint: You cannot force a man to be a man. This is especially true if he didn't grow up with a male role model. There is no miracle that a woman can perform that will make up for a lifetime of having his masculine instincts dulled by a domineering single mother.

A Coon in Disguise

I once knew a couple, we'll call them Maria and Antoine, who came together for the sole purpose of splitting bills 50/50. They agreed to respect each other and be faithful in a "friends with benefits" type of relationship. Things started out okay, but obviously this type of arrangement was destined to fail. Antoine began having child support from a previous union withheld from his check, which meant he could no longer split the bills 50/50. His name was on the lease, so Maria couldn't put him out. They continued on with the relationship as well as they could.

Maria began to notice that Antoine started wearing new clothes on a regular basis. Where was this stuff coming from? He was always overly friendly with sisters, but it was getting much worse. It became quite clear where he was getting this extra money. It was also evident that none of it was going to helping pay bills. Maria began paying attention to the changes in his schedule and taking count of missing condoms. She wasn't too concerned about his actions because as soon as the lease was up, she planned to leave. Unfortunately, that was still in the distant future. Time went on and they began to lead semi-separate lives. Maria worked overtime to save up for her move. She continued to utilize Antoine from time to time, because she was not the type to go jumping from man to man. It seemed better to just use the raggedy one she had for the time being. Why not? Everyone else was.

A few months before the lease was up she began noticing strange things. To begin with, there was a Caucasian female named Becky who began taking Antoine to work. He claimed it was a new carpool project at his job. Because he lived nearby he was first on the pickup list. He assured Maria the woman was a lesbian, which was believable. Becky was horrendously ugly and built like a refrigerator. Occasionally he would be bold enough to invite her in to hang out, usually with his other friends. Maria would always kick her out because she didn't like Caucasians in her home.

One day, she had a weird feeling while she was at work. She felt as though something wasn't right at home. Could it be the white girl? It better not be! She left work early to see what was going on. As she walked in the door she saw Antoine sitting in her bedroom surfing the web. She was relieved, no Becky hanging around. As Maria said hello, there were two hellos returned. As she walked to the bedroom she saw his friend Rob sitting on her bed putting on his shoes. That was weird. They explained they were in her room just trying to find some information on something, as they went in the living room.

A few weeks later Maria was cleaning the apartment. They each had their own bathroom and bedroom since it was a fairly large unit and they both liked their space. She never cleaned his rooms, especially since he wasn't handling his share of the bills. Be that as it may, it was a crisp autumn afternoon and she was in a good mood. She decided to straighten up his bathroom since it was so close to the main entrance. As she cleaned she complained about all the junk he had in there. She had to move it just to be able to wipe down the surfaces. As she moved some papers, something told her to read them. She put them down because she didn't believe in violating people's privacy, but something said **read them**! Against her better judgment she began to read a letter. It was from Becky. It was page after page explaining how Maria was a crazy Black chick who didn't know how to love him or take care of him. It said that Becky would always be his *"bottom bitch."*

She caught the gist of the letter but had to phone a friend for the definition of *"bottom bitch."* Once that was cleared up, she lost it. She could ignore some of the sisters he cheated with, but a white girl? A repulsively ugly, shapeless white girl? A white girl who he brought in her house? That was unforgivable. She immediately decided to jump online and find a way to make this situation right. Maria devised a plan to splice an electrical cord, plug it in and connect it to the metal door knob. She couldn't find out if there was enough voltage to do enough damage though. Also, if she was successful, how could she dispose of 230 lbs. of charred Negro? Luckily she chose to call her friend back to fine-tune her plans. Instead, the friend talked her down, though it took a quite a few hours of intense intervention.

Needless to say, realizing that you are about to go to jail over a lowlife is a good reason to end things. Maria later saw Antoine's friend Rob and asked him if there was ever any down-low activity going on. He said, "Of course not!" But he was looking down and away when he said it. She'll never really know, but she will always have her suspicions.

When it becomes clear you can't trust a male, it may be best to end the relationship. Without a firm foundation of trust, you have nothing.

The Fraud

I once knew a beautiful family who seemed to have it all. We'll call them Steven and Janice. Steven was a respected minister. Janice had a prestigious job working for the city. They had been married for many years and were held in high esteem. They owned a nice home deep in the suburbs with two beautiful children.

Steven's success made him very arrogant. His wife was book smart but didn't have an ounce of common sense. That is just how he liked it. Steven would counsel people from all across the country, but never bothered to preach his doctrine too strongly in his own home. His philosophy was that men should marry "dumb women". If your wife didn't know a lot about your beliefs, she wouldn't be able to argue with you and hold you accountable for wrongdoing. When he mentioned this to me in a conversation, I knew he was a shady character.

Stephen began traveling around the country, usually leaving his family at home. He was rumored to have had a few adulterous indiscretions. No one had any actual proof of any immorality, so it was never addressed in the community. As time went on he began having less intimate contact with Janice. She caught him watching smut on several occasions and didn't understand why he didn't just come to her the way he used to. He tried to avoid sexual intercourse but she began pushing the issue.

One day she felt excruciating pain around her genitals. She examined herself and things didn't look right to her. She went to the doctor and was diagnosed with a severe sexually transmitted disease. It was then that she put two and two together. Stephen had known for some time that he was carrying this disease and was trying his best to avoid passing it to her. He used porn as a release so he wouldn't need to make love to Janice. It was on an occasion when Janice insisted on having sex that she was infected. She felt betrayed and to make it worse, she was in constant indescribable pain. It angered her that he didn't just humble himself and admit the truth instead of exposing her to harm. He didn't want to lose the façade of his perfect life. If a man's disloyalty puts your life or health in jeopardy and you don't want to work it out, you are not wrong to leave.

Abandonment

My last story is about a couple I'll call Tasha and Thomas. Tasha was still a teenager when she met Thomas. She was inexperienced and excited about finding such a smart, industrious older man who was interested in her. They got along well and were together for years. They never got legally married because he didn't believe that "the man" needed to give him permission to marry a wife. They never actually moved in together either, because he liked his privacy and didn't feel the need to follow what he considered Western norms.

He had a couple of children with other women over the years. Tasha accepted them because Thomas was her first sexual experience and she did not want to leave. She was deeply "in love". She treated his children well and never made them feel resented. She did whatever she could to help him with his business ventures. She hoped he would appreciate her effort and one day be repay her by being faithful.

One month her period was late. She was surprised, but not worried. Could this mean she would have one of his babies? If so, would he be willing to make a real commitment to her now? She took the test and it was positive. She was so happy. When he came over that night she told him she was expecting his baby. Instead of being thrilled he was angry. He said he had enough mouths to feed and accused her of trying to trap him. He boldly told her to get rid of the baby or their relationship would be over. She was stunned and confused. Why was it such a big deal when he allowed other women to have his children? What was more important, the relationship or her baby? She went back and forth in her mind. Thomas became more and more hostile as weeks passed. She finally made the decision to abort the pregnancy.

Afterwards she was crushed. She felt a void inside where life once grew. Had she really murdered her own child? The next time she saw Thomas she told him she had the abortion. He told her she had really caused him a lot of stress recently. In the meantime he had met another woman who wouldn't take him "through the motions". He was leaving her for good. Tasha felt like a complete fool for killing her child.

Helpful Hint: If your man refuses to make a solid commitment to you or abandons his family, you are not wrong to leave. Never let a man play around with you. He should either be all

the way in or all the way out. He should not have the choice of being your man in his spare time. You are worth far more than that.

These are all examples of when there is very little that can be fixed. There are times when things have just gone too far. There is a line that can be crossed which marks a point of no return. Don't waste time trying to save something that isn't salvageable. What you can focus on is how to avoid this happening again. How do you make better choices next time?

Mate Selection

Mate selection is the best predictor of the longevity in your relationship. Contrary to popular belief, opposites don't attract, at least not long term. There has to be a basic foundation upon which you agree. There must be common goals, positions and motives to keep you from drifting apart. If you decide to leave your current relationship, you owe it to yourself to make a better selection next time. Realize your own value and be sure that whoever you choose realizes your value as well.

When selecting a mate, remember the role of a man is to protect, provide and guide. Can this man do all three? Two out of three won't work. He has to be able to do them all. This is not something you can compromise on. When I say provide, I do not mean extravagance. I mean basic food, clothing, shelter and a few niceties. A man should be able to give these things to you whether you choose to work outside the home or not. He should be protective, even mildly territorial over you and his children. A potential mate should definitely have the wisdom to guide you. If he is less intelligent than you it will not be a good match.

Men are able to run game on women much easier than they can run it on another man. Seek the advice of an elder, preferably a man before making a decision. Sometimes love and lust can blind you. Listen closely and strongly consider what these advisors say.

Premature sex ruins the chances of making a good decision. You should hold off physical intimacy until the commitment is finalized. Before that point you are only <u>considering</u> being with this man. **He has not earned the right to be with you in that way.** We have been desensitized about how serious sex is. A woman allows her man into the deepest, most intimate part of herself when making love. She takes in his energy, whether it is good or bad. She connects to him. She may even bring forth new life. Do not randomly give yourself away.

If it gets hard to wait, turn off the television and stop listening to popular music. The media bombards us with sexual innuendo. Try listening to world, jazz or classical music. There is nothing wrong with broadening your tastes. Begin watching documentaries. This will give you more interesting (non-sexual) things to discuss. Don't talk about sex or you will end up wanting to do it. Once your mind starts going there, the body will surely follow. Pray or meditate often. Focus on laying the groundwork for a fulfilling future. Do not meet the man in private places. Always be in public or with other company until you are both ready to commit.

Investigate him. Be sure the things he has told you are true. For instance, don't take his word for it when he complains about his "baby momma". There are always two sides to a story. Talk to her as well. If you settle down with this man you will have to deal with her regularly so you might as well get it out of the way. Always keep in mind that she may lie to try to keep you apart, but listen discerningly anyway. Talk to his mother, his grandmother, his sisters and his aunts. What do they say about him? What kinds of friends does he have? Does he have a criminal record? What's his credit rating? How do you fit into his schedule? Be aware of these things.

Find a man who you like as-is. Do not get with a man with the intention to change him. This doesn't work. It will make him resent you and disrupt any chance of peace. A man wants to be accepted just like you do. Don't look at a man's potential. Look at the reality. Love him as he is or leave him alone.

A Note on Physical Violence

No intelligent man should hit a woman. There is always a better way to handle a situation than stooping to putting your hands on someone. That being said, sisters need to watch their mouths. I have heard women say things to men and thought to myself, "He is better than I am because I would've punched her in her mouth if she said that to me." White feminists are quick to place all the blame on a man in these situations. As a Black woman, I know better.

Everyone must take responsibility for their actions. Just as a man must refrain from using his superior strength and power against belligerent women, women must control the insulting things we say to men. This is not a one sided issue. Black women hate to admit their role in these things, but we do play a major part. Luckily, I do not know what it is like to be hit by a man, not even my father. I make mistakes in communication, but not to the point of walking around with black eyes and busted lips! Be respectful. As I said earlier, you are life partners, not sparring partners.

If a man hits you often or is genuinely abusive, it is a reasonable decision to leave. In fact it is imperative to go! Don't leave yourself open to be roughed up or seriously injured by a monster. **If your man abuses your children you should not hesitate to leave.** It is your duty to protect your offspring.

Nonetheless, if you know your mouth is out of control causing you to demean him, disrespect his pride and trample on his manhood on a regular basis, then you should work on that before completely giving up. I'm not going to tell you what a talk show psychologist would tell you. I'm going to keep it real. If you both work on your weaknesses, it may be salvageable. You know best.

Never put yourself or your children in harm's way.

Chapter Twelve: Review

- In healthy relationships men and women gladly serve each other. Women serve men by providing comfort in various ways. Men serve women through protection, security and sustenance, among other things. Both roles are intertwined and equally necessary. Never be ashamed to be in service to your man. Devotion is a beautiful virtue.
- Most men are happy as long as they have a clean home, peace and quiet, tasty food and physical satisfaction. They have very simple desires, unlike us. You don't have to jump through hoops to keep your man happy. Just be sure those basics are covered.
- Many times we get into a relationship and stop pursuing our own interests and hobbies. This can make you quite dissatisfied with your life as well as cause you to be a bore. Continue to pursue your interests, study and make time for yourself. You can't bring joy to your family if you are not fulfilled and happy within.
- Let everyone who enters your home feel the genuine love and contentment. Many times they might not have any of their own. To be able to share yours is a blessing.
- Words have power, but so does silence. Everything doesn't require a response. You don't always have to have the last word. Sometimes silence speaks louder much than words.
- Due to our history in this country, Black men crave respect more than any other group of people. Always show the utmost respect in conversations. Always acknowledge that whatever he is saying is relevant and important.
- Never be afraid to admit you are wrong. Acknowledging wrong doesn't show weakness, it shows maturity and makes a man feel respected.
- Never argue in public! I repeat, never argue in public or in front of guests. We all make mistakes but do not allow yourself to be knocked off your pedestal. Use creativity instead of aggression. He will love you for it.
- Avoid using emasculating words like "little" when referring to him, his ideas or his accomplishments. Little is not a very manly word and tends to minimize him and his accomplishments. It

- sounds insulting. Instead use words like "big" or "great". It makes a difference.
- Men and women are 100% equal in terms of their value and rights. However, rights are different than authority. You are not equal in terms of authority. Your input is valued, but his decision is final.
- There are ways to express your views and get your way at home. In most circumstances, direct confrontation and rebellion are not productive!
- If you just sit around complaining about not being satisfied without doing anything to improve your condition, you are being lazy. If you are lazy, he might not be pleased with your performance either. Maybe he's just too nice to express it. If you don't like how he's making love to you, try making love to him.
- Using sex as a weapon is a horrible idea. The desire to use sex as a weapon says a lot about you and your relationship. Women use sex as a weapon for many reasons, none of them good or productive.
- Cleanliness is next to Godliness. You must NEVER overlook this aspect of lovemaking. There is nothing worse than being near a woman who smells like fish instead of flowers. It is very offensive and can make you lose respect for that woman. Bad body odors are very unladylike.
- If you want to keep peace in your relationship, always dress your daughters modestly. Good fathers hate to see little girls, especially their own, dressed provocatively.
- Helpful Hint: Diamonds are stored away because jewelers don't want masses of people having access to their most valuable pieces. This is true of all prized possessions. You are worth more than a shiny rock. Act like it! Covering your body shows respect for your man and it protects him as well.
- The easiest and most effective thing you can do to improve your appearance is to smile! Many Black women have extremely mean, uninviting expressions on their faces the majority of the time. Make an effort to look friendly and happy. Use your smile to brighten up your family's day!
- Unless he understands and respects the gift of heaven between your legs, do not allow any man to enter your vagina. Good

women respect their womb, spirit and integrity too much to cheat or be promiscuous.
- You cannot force a man to be a man. This is especially true if he didn't grow up with a male role model. There is no miracle that a woman can perform that will make up for a lifetime of having his masculine instincts dulled by a domineering single mother.
- If your man refuses to make a solid commitment to you or abandons his family, you are not wrong to leave. Never let a man play around with you. He should either be all the way in or all the way out. He should not have the choice of being your man in his spare time. You are worth far more than that.

Chapter Thirteen: Conclusion

Rest assured, if there are still common interests and true love in your relationship it is possible to salvage it. And even if your relationship is good, you can make it great! Most Black people find it challenging to create healthy long-term relationships, but that is by design! It is not our fault. Our years of enslavement and brainwashing in this land have crippled us emotionally and socially. However, just as we were taught to be dysfunctional, we can learn to be balanced again. Practice makes perfect!

I love you and wish you nothing but happiness in your family! I pray that you can learn lessons from this book which will allow you to avoid common pitfalls. I offer this advice not because I was born wise, but because I've wasted a lot of time making mistakes. Learn from my errors and observations. Black people have suffered long enough. We deserve to love and be loved. We are worthy of security and trust. We have earned the right to be whole again. Black people come from an amazingly charismatic, loving and strong people. All we have to do is remember who we are and act accordingly.

I wrote this book in a very general way to make it applicable to every Black survivor of racism on the planet. We are all seeking love, affection, respect, stability and healing. Although none of my suggestions are extremely difficult, they do take time to master. Changing the way we think and being willing to go against the oppressive cultural perspectives which were forced upon us takes determination. That being said, if you are disciplined enough to implement the lessons in this book I assure you your life will begin to change.

I am honored you took the time to read my words. The next step is to apply these principles to your life. Let's be the best women we can possibly be. Begin by giving your man a big hug and apologizing for your part in harming the relationship. You now have the tools to start building it back up. Best wishes!

For more information from the author:

http://www.authorangelafreeman.com

Author's Facebook Page:

https://www.facebook.com/wmstblog

God's Gift Facebook Page: **https://www.facebook.com/GodsGiftBook**

Be on the lookout for the upcoming book from Angela Freeman entitled "**Conscious Entertaining: The Return of the Domestic Goddess**".

Special Thanks Goes To:

First and most importantly, I give a sincere thank you to The Honorable Elijah Muhammad (pbuh) for teaching me absolutely everything that I know of value. I would have nothing worth saying if I hadn't been awakened by your words.

Mark "Hannibal" Pastor, if I lived a thousand lifetimes I could never thank you enough for creating such a unique and warm environment that everyone could go to for mental nourishment. It was at Artistic Apparel I began my quest for knowledge and Nationalism as a young girl. The city has not been the same since you've been gone. Rest in Uhuru.

Special thanks to my WOH/United Front family, thanks for giving me inspiration when I needed it most. IG & Nefertari gave me renewed faith by showing me there are a few people left who are not willing to compromise. I have learned so much from each of you. I could never repay the debt. Your influence has transformed me into a better and stronger person. This book would not have come to fruition without help from my big brothers IG, O, True & Bomani (you treat me bad, bruh lol).

To my Brother Mapinduzi Mwandishi, who I doubt actually exists in real life; thank you for your input, guidance and support!

Ahmad Muhammad aka Rudy X Harlow (pbuh) & Brother Shabazz of NYC I sincerely thank you both for keeping my mind focused and being true brothers.

Thank you to Dr. Khallid Muhammad (pbuh) for showing me how to stand up and speak the truth without fear. You are missed.

Thanks to everyone who supported my blog, radio program and this book! Your encouragement keeps me motivated to explore new endeavors. I'm honored you find this information beneficial. Please keep showing me love.

Thank you so much to everyone who volunteered to have their reflections embellish this book. It added a lot. You are all beautiful representations of Black womanhood!

Thank you to my parents and grandparents who raised me from a cute, hard headed little girl into an absolutely adorable, hard headed woman. I appreciate the DNA!

Lastly, a million thanks goes to my husband who inspired me to be better, love stronger and laugh harder. He is the only man who ever awakened the desire in me to become a better woman. And he's fine too! I love you ChiChi!